COCOON

COCOON

How One Woman Created a
Shelter for Teens and Found
Hope Along the Way

Sarri Gilman

Cherish
EDITIONS

Published in 2023 by Cherish Editions
An imprint of Shaw Callaghan Ltd
UK Office
The Stanley Building
7 Pancras Square
Kings Cross
London N1C 4AG

US Office
On Point Executive Center, Inc
3030 N. Rocky Point Drive W.
Suite 150
Tampa, FL 33607
www.triggerhub.org

A CIP catalogue record for this book is available upon request
from the British Library
ISBN: 978-1-915680-61-7
Ebook ISBN: 978-1-915680-62-4

Typeset by Lapiz Digital Services
Cover design by More Visual

CONTENTS

For my daughters, who live by their values. We walked this road together, your hands always in mine. My home will always be where you are.

For my husband who caught me in midair and taught me that I did not have to earn love. Thank you for laying the foundation of constancy, for being gentle, wise and using love as your guidance system. For our family together, I am grateful.

I have tried to recreate events, locales and conversations from my memories of them. In order to maintain their anonymity, I have changed the names of individuals in some instances. I may have changed some identifying characteristics and details, such as physical properties, occupations and places of residence. I have also left out certain individuals when it would be too confusing to add new people into the story for a single sentence.

The conversations in the book all come from my recollections, though they are not written to represent word-for-word transcripts. Instead, I retold them in a way that evokes the feeling and meaning of what was said, and in all instances, the essence of the dialogue is accurate.

Even with these minor changes, the story you are about to read is true.

1

FEATHERS

New York
1964

When you've been abandoned as a child, you're left with half a self. You must try to figure out how to earn love, how to stop the wounded half-self from ripping open, and how to make yourself whole.

My early childhood memories were of small things, fragments, like when you find a feather on the ground: You know that feather came from a bird that flew by.

I remember the blanket on my bed, pink and white with a picture of a girl with dark hair. I imagined the girl on my blanket was a princess who lived in a castle.

I had a pet turtle who fit in my hand. He had a plastic container with a tiny pond to swim in and a rock mound for drying off.

I had a Pinocchio puppet and Little Red Riding Hood. My father made puppet shows with me in bed before I went to sleep under the princess blanket. I believed the thumb-sized Mouseketeer children lived in my square black-and-white television.

I ran down the hall to the room where my new baby brother slept. Adam was my baby. I wanted to hold him and carry him around.

My mother gave me a swaddled bundle to hold if I sat very still. I rocked him, I sang to him.

And then I peeked behind the blanket.

To my horror my baby brother had become a frozen-faced doll. Adam wasn't in the blanket.

I'd lost Adam.

I screamed in panic.

I can still feel my knees melt, my breath stop in my chest, the plunge into terror.

I lived with this terrible fear of losing my brother. As a young child, I took him everywhere with me.

He was the feather I picked up from the ground.

He was the only thing that remained.

***

Everett, Washington
2014

It was an hour before noon; I parked my car across the street from the convention center on Hewitt in downtown Everett. It was a sunny day. I wore a short-sleeved black dress, no jewelry and black ballet shoes. A shawl I'd knitted, pink-pearl and mauve, was wrapped around my shoulders, and it felt like my sanctuary, holding me together as I was about to do something that would take me back into the trenches. My hair was dark, long and wavy. It swallowed my face unless it was pulled back in a clip. Though my glasses helped me see, they couldn't help me remember all the names. I was arriving early so I could take in the scene before the hundreds of guests arrived. I wanted a few minutes to listen to my memories whisper in my ear.

As I walked toward the entrance of the convention center, the sunlight was glowing around a group of teens. Girls in their dresses — bright colors, black lace, puffy skirts, silk bows around their waists — were awkward in their heels and makeup. The teen boys were seeing each other wearing suits, white shirts and ties for the first time. Some wore sneakers and some wore new, still-uncomfortable shoes. They were laughing, joking, their bodies jittery and nervous, as if they would float off any minute into the sky like untethered balloons. Adults approached the teens in groups of two and three, offering compliments, telling them how nice they looked. I hugged my shawl tighter around my shoulders as I watched the kids stand up taller, grinning as the adults' words sank in.

There is nothing like watching a kid stand up taller.

I continued into the convention hall, past the teens and their staff, who were hugging them and encouraging them. I wanted to hug them too, but I didn't know any of these kids. I was a stranger. The kids I knew were grown.

***

Years ago, I didn't know anyone in this town. I hadn't grown up here, didn't even have the most important credential: graduation from Everett High. I didn't know the difference between a Douglas fir and a cedar. I couldn't tell if the wind was coming down from the north or up from the south. I shivered in the persistent rain that softens to mist and fog so heavy you can't tell if it's raining or not. I pronounced the names of the nearby towns all wrong. I wasn't aware of the shift-change schedule at the Boeing plant. I didn't like the taste of salmon. I hadn't grown up taking a bus to a farm to pick berries in the summer. I didn't know how to catch a crab. Soaring red-tailed hawks, owl calls at night, fledging herons, the way momma deer park their babies in your yard for you to babysit — it was all new to me. Home isn't always where you come from. It's sometimes a place you've never been.

The glistening new convention hall, windows and steel sweeping upward, had been built for special occasions where the leaders and dignitaries of the town took center stage. Today, it was for the jittery kids. And though I did not know the kids standing outside the convention center, there was a thread connecting us, timeless and unbreakable.

I couldn't help but think of Holli.

It had taken years to gain the spiritual perspective to see how she had saved thousands of kids. Now, on the threshold of the gleaming convention hall, I could make peace with what had happened. Back then, all I could feel was desperation.

2

HOLLI

Everett, Washington
1990

Holli was sleeping under my desk. In my tiny counseling office at the school, there was barely enough room for the two of us.

Still, the office where Holli squeezed under my desk was one of the nicer school offices I'd had. There was a window that looked over the street. My door opened to the main office where the school secretary cheerfully greeted teens and staff with Hershey's Kisses from the candy dish on her desk, decorated with a bright yellow smiley face.

The principal was next door to me, which was handy, as I often needed to run something by him. Besides, having worked in a few schools, I was used to being given office spaces the size of an airplane bathroom. I'd once worked as a counselor from the broom closet of a middle school.

This school was not your typical public school. This was a school for kids on probation, kids who had served time in detention, often many times – repeat "offenders." Our school was an outpost, tucked inside of a two-story building in downtown Everett. It wasn't designed to be a school; it was an office building, suitable for adults who wore ties, behaved in elevators and didn't throw chewing gum wherever they damn well pleased.

The school population was 70 teenagers, more boys than girls, and each kid carried heavy problems to school – problems no kid could solve.

Holli was often sleeping in my office. She had glued herself to me. In a school like this, having a kid stick to you was a good thing. The kids had so little in their lives, they needed adults they felt attached to. While Holli slept under my desk, I would sometimes leave my office and unlock an empty classroom to see other kids. I would stick a sign on my door that said "HOLLI." Then, the school secretary and principal knew she was under my desk or in my chair.

Holli was often up walking the streets at night. She was avoiding the evening parade of men her mother brought home. Holli had long, thin, light brown hair. She was 17 years old, but seemed much younger, more like an 11-year-old. Her mascara was gooped on her tiny lashes, which left dark blotches under her wide, brown eyes.

It had been early in the morning when she came to my door, wiping away tears and mascara. She told me she was going to her "place," which meant under my desk. Holli rarely told me about how things went at home. But this day was different. The tears were my opening.

I closed my door for privacy. "Holli, what happened?"

I didn't know if she would answer – some things are too hard to talk about. And I carried many things inside, buried deep. I was certain no one would ever hear me say those things aloud. I respected silence.

I would wait with my question.

This day, she would open her door.

Her words floated one by one, slowly, as if she were in a dream. She described a man her mother brought home. He'd cornered her in the bathroom. He'd ripped her shirt.

Then her dream ended.

She said she was never going back home.

Holli's home was in a dilapidated part of town, a motel full of cheap rooms rented by the hour or month. Nearby bars were open day and night.

Holli closed her eyes and drew her knees up tight against her chest.

I knew not to ask questions. Her eyes were closed. She said all she could. I took my jacket off the back of my chair and laid it over her shivering knees. She wasn't cold – she was traumatized.

I called Child Protective Services for the third time about Holli. The law required me, as a counselor, to call Child Protective Services every time I heard from a child about a threat to their safety, or about abuse or harm to them from their parents or grandparents, whoever they lived with. If I didn't make the reports, I could lose my license. The teenagers I worked with were often hit, thrown out of their homes and not fed. I had a stack of calls to make every week to Child Protective Services. They never sent a worker to investigate a single call.

I usually wrote out my words before making a call. Maybe if I said just the right ones, they would come. Sometimes I pleaded with the person taking my call: "Please, please send someone." Other times I was demanding.

"Repeat back to me what I just said," wanting proof that my report was being written somewhere. Over time I learned to just be neutral, do my job, make the report, note that I made the report and expect nothing.

Child Protective Services was underfunded and understaffed, with only a few workers to cover 277 miles along Interstate 5 in Washington State. They had to prioritize the youngest, most fragile, vulnerable kids. I had a school full of teenagers on probation. The school was nicknamed "The Dumpster." The kids weren't seen as vulnerable; they were labeled "criminal." The teens in my school didn't seem as vulnerable as, say, a three-year-old in a daycare center with a bruised neck.

After waiting on hold, I gave information about Holli, making my mandated report. The person on the phone asked if I could stick around for two to three hours. A Child Protective Services worker would come and interview Holli. I was shocked and relieved. I didn't know what magic words I had spoken, but Child Protective Services was sending someone.

I wondered if I should line up all the other kids while I had the Child Protective Services worker in the building, but thought, "No, that would just distract from Holli. Focus on the one."

"Just one. If only we could save one." That was my mantra.

In my mind, I was getting Holli to safety. Child Protective Services was going to swoop in and give Holli a home. She would have a bedroom with a bed of her own, instead of a couch in a motel room. She'd have a foster mom that made her breakfast. I sat in my fantasy, feeling hope and relief.

I called home and asked the babysitter to stay a few extra hours with my daughters. I never got home late, but this was an exception. I wanted to stay and witness the miracle. I also didn't want Holli to be alone when she met with the social worker, a stranger who she wouldn't trust. She needed someone familiar by her side.

Within two hours, the school secretary popped her head in and told me the Child Protective Services worker had arrived. I jumped up to meet her.

Mary, the Child Protective Services worker, said hello while she was unwrapping her chocolate kiss. She had on glasses and a knit hat, polyester pants and a bright yellow blouse with bold-colored shapes printed all over it. The shapes reminded me of little kids and all their different shapes and sizes. Mary's job – the job of every Child Protective Services worker – was to watch over kids, check on their safety, and if they weren't safe, get them to a placement: a foster home or group home. Mary had the power to get Holli out of the motel room where she lived with her mom. Mary alone could say, "You are coming with me."

Mary looked about 20 years older than me, wiser and more experienced. I was 28 years old, a new mom with twin babies, learning how to deal with croup, diaper rash, ear infections and teething. I did not know how to help Holli get out of the terrifying motel room.

Mary wanted to meet alone with Holli. I wanted to sit in, but Mary gave me a look that told me we were going to do this her way.

I opened the door to my office.

"She's under there."

I pointed to Holli under my desk.

"I'll wake her up," I said, crawling on my hands and knees. I was certain Holli was awake and just keeping her eyes shut. Her reluctance to open her eyes was not a good start.

I got Holli to raise herself into a chair, and I left. I stood in the hallway. In less than five minutes, my door opened, and Mary walked out with her worn, experienced briefcase in one hand and her coat over her other arm. Holli was in the chair.

"What happened?" I asked Mary.

"Holli said no." Mary continued walking. She went down the stairs to the door of the school.

I followed.

"Wait. Where are you going? You can't just leave her on the streets. She will be raped, beaten. Terrible things are going to happen to her."

Mary stopped and pointed her chin at me, her face taut.

"Tell me something I don't know."

She pushed open the door to the school and kept walking.

"Wait, please." I followed Mary into the parking lot across the street. She kept moving. I felt the anger boiling up inside my stomach. I wasn't some kid sleeping under a desk. I wanted to discuss the situation, and I wanted Child Protective Services to do something. I wanted Holli to leave with Mary.

"Isn't there a shelter you can send her to?"

"No such thing. The shelters don't take any kid without a parent, and they don't even take a teenager with a parent."

"What do you mean, they won't take a teenager into a shelter with their parent?"

"You heard me. No one over the age of 11." Mary lost patience with my stupidity. I was getting angry. There was an edge in my voice. "Can't you take her somewhere safe?" Mary heard my edge and snapped at me.

"Not if she doesn't want to go. She said NO. I have no more time for a kid that doesn't want to go with me, and I have no more time to explain this to you. Get this in your head: I don't have any place to take her anyway. She'd just be driving around in my car with me all day and then sleeping in a chair in my office. We don't have placements for all the kids."

And at that moment, heartbreak overwhelmed the anger inside me.

I watched Mary toss her tattered briefcase into her trunk. She opened her car door. I thought about all the kids she would have to see that day, the ones who were battered enough to get into her car with her.

I knew Mary was just doing her job. I stood there as the car pulled away, feeling like a little kid who had just been dumped. The parking lot was filled with pigeon shit, which I tried to avoid as I walked back to the school.

I did not have time to listen to the little girl inside of me. She would have to wait until later.

But I felt her standing on my lungs, making it hard to breathe.

I yanked the heavy school door open, dragged myself up the stairs and returned to my desk. I wiped tears from my face, hoping no one in the office noticed. I sat at my desk, turning a pencil between my fingers over and over like a baton. I was thinking.

Holli was in her last class of the day, social studies.

I twirled my pencil.

I opened the phone book and called every one of the eight shelters listed.

"Do you take teenagers? Seventeen-year-olds? Sixteen, fourteen-year-olds?" I wondered if age made a difference. Maybe they would take pity on a fourteen-year-old.

Every single place I called said no.

When I asked why, I got vague answers. "State law." "Too much liability." "Teens are too difficult." I wasn't sure what they meant. I understood that teens could be difficult. But it left me with a lot to think about.

There were no open doors for a kid.

The school bell buzzed. It was time for me to go home, and time for Holli to go God-knows-where.

I drove off to catch my ferry and see my baby twin daughters, Somer and Aliza.

I missed my baby girls when I was at the school. Usually, I left the school at noon and was home for the afternoons and evenings with my babies. I wasn't trying to balance working and mothering. I was a mommy. That was my full-time role. My daughters were nine months old. I was only trying to get a few hours of work in each week, *around* being a mommy. I saw a few people in private practice and worked a few hours in the school.

Because of Mary and Holli, I was returning on the 4pm ferry instead of the 1 o'clock.

I had missed the afternoon with my baby girls for nothing.

When I got home, I scooped both my girls into my arms, burying my nose in their fine, honey-colored hair. I carried Somer and Aliza, one on each hip, to the nursery to get their matching woolen sweaters (made by my mother-in-law, Ruth). I laid my sweatered daughters side by side. I picked up Aliza and carried her out to the porch, where the breeze coming up from the south cooled the air. I fastened her into her yellow swing. I jogged back into the house to fetch Somer. Socrates, our German shepherd and my companion of eight years, ran ahead of me on the way back to the porch. Our dog was like a nanny. Wherever the babies went, she went. She never left them.

Socrates lay down on the wooden porch while I pushed my laughing daughters in their swings. I looked out over Puget Sound; I could see Everett across the water.

I didn't know if I wanted to go back to the school. Some part of me felt like I wasn't helping anyone. But I couldn't just not show up. I was someone to Holli and the other kids. They didn't have other adults showing up for them. Our school was where adults showed up.

I looked out across the water of Puget Sound to the Cascade Range. I was doing laps in my head, hearing all the ways the shelters said no.

My twins were ready for a story. Their tiny, puffy hands were chilly. Back inside we went to warm up and read *The Runaway Bunny* by Margaret Wise Brown. It always made me cry. The baby bunny says it will run away and turn into all these different things, and the mommy bunny says, "I will always find you."

"I will be a bird and fly away from you," said the little bunny.

"If you will be a bird and fly away from me, I will be a tree you come home to," says the mother bunny.

The story was a prayer I was reciting: "You will always belong to me. I will never lose you."

My daughters were too young to understand. But the little girl inside of me – the one standing on my chest earlier in the day – could sit on her cozy reading pillow in my daughters' nursery, snuggling with stuffed animals in the periwinkle-and-creamy-yellow color scheme, while an old cedar tree leaned over the window, and I read aloud.

I promised my daughters I would become the mother I never had.

3

PAUL

Whidbey Island, WA

I was working with Holli because I had followed my mentor Paul to the Everett school. Paul was a school principal. Taller than most people, he was Sasquatch in button-down plaid shirts and slacks. He also stood for things that were big. He stood for kids who struggled to make it to school each day. He stood for kids who were failing classes. He stood for relationships rather than scholastic requirements.

Paul and I first met on Whidbey Island. I was a stranger in a community where he'd known everyone and their families for two decades. He'd finished building a new high school. I'd just moved up from Los Angeles to the Pacific Northwest and was looking for a teaching job.

It wasn't a planned move. I'd been on a three-day holiday and caught the ferry to the island for lunch. When I got off, I'd rented a cabin, put my marriage and job on ice, and stayed. I returned to LA only to get my dog Socrates and my pet rabbit.

I bunked down in a one-room cabin, no mail service or phone. No immediate neighbors, just my German shepherd and rabbit as companions and a small cassette player. Cedar trees, hemlock and Douglas firs surrounded the cabin. If I wanted to talk to someone, I had to drive a few miles to a payphone on the highway.

I stopped by the high school to ask about a job and leave my resume. The door to the school was open, but no one was in the office. There was a light on behind a glass door that said "PRINCIPAL" in gold letters. The school felt empty; a fresh paint smell lingered in the air. I called out, "Hello?" to the glass door. The guy sitting behind it yelled, "Come on in."

I guess my resume told Paul everything he needed to know. I'd worked with teens tagged "severely emotionally disturbed." After working with LA kids who had carried assault weapons to school, set fires in a classroom and knocked a teacher unconscious with a chair, I had the chops to work with hard-to-reach kids.

Paul hired me on the spot as a counselor, one day a week. Since I was a stranger, I knew I was lucky to get even a single day a week of work.

I settled in. The island was a contrast to Los Angeles. People on the island stopped to talk in the grocery store. They went out of their way to show me how make a wood fire, catch trout, dig for clams. The stores were selling ordinary, useful things; no one was trying to impress anyone. The miles of beach, billowing clouds and gentle mist they called "rain" dazzled me. The evergreen trees felt like guardians: protective, strong, sheltering.

When school started, I looked forward to my hours each week at the school. Paul awed me. He laughed easily and helped me not be too hard on myself. He joked around and was childish in the pranks he pulled on all the staff. It was his way of letting each of us know he liked us and thought of us enough to organize some crazy prank on us. He made us all feel like kids. He got us to be what the teens needed us to be.

In my mind, Paul was a god among school leaders.

I never saw him suspend a kid. I never saw him give up on a kid. I don't know how Paul ever got to the principal stuff on his desk, because I never saw him doing paperwork. Paul conversed with students, staff, parents, community members and anyone who walked into the school. If I needed to find Paul, I would start with the halls, then the lunchroom, looking last in his office.

As I spent my Fridays at the island high school, Paul found more and more kids for me to work with, and we added Wednesdays and Thursdays. Then, we added younger kids at the middle school.

The kids Paul sent to me had losses, like the loss of a parent or a sibling. Lives disrupted by moves, by an assault at home from a drunk parent. They were survivors of their family shipwrecks. They all carried secrets. School was the reliable place. But for the kids, it was also a lonely place.

I gave the kids magazines they could tear up and make collages. I had a jar filled with single words cut out from the magazines – they could pour out the words and arrange them into poems. We used watercolor paper, soft to the touch, and brushes and clean water to dip and splash about the page. They poured colored sand in layers in jars and watched the colors form designs. They worked on an unfinished jigsaw puzzle.

Glue was the most important ingredient for the work of counseling teens. It is, of course, for repairing things and putting things back together. Hot glue for puzzles. (After all the effort of putting them together, some kids couldn't bear taking them apart.) Glue sticks for collaging and not getting sticky fingers. (It made teens feel more in control.) Elmer's glue for the smell. (It made us feel childlike and open to trying something new and messy.) Superglue for everything else.

When your life has come apart, glue is a useful thing to have around.

A kid could always find something to do in my office, some excuse to enter and sit at the table and talk.

Their searching faces would open my door and chirp, "Is the puzzle still here?" "Could I get fresh water to paint?" "Got anything for me to do?"

I left things out to serve as lures, to give a kid a reason to see me and finish something they were working on in my room. But we both knew it was a chance to bring some stories out of their caves – the dark places where they were hiding them.

They were afraid to tell their stories. I would bring them warmth, sit with them in what they were facing, cleanse wounds, listen to their feelings, quiet the fears, help them stand up and walk out of the darkness into the daylight.

So, when they went back to class, they were no longer stuffing everything in. They had taken it out, unpacked it, glued the broken bits together and left the worst of it with me.

I was happy working in the school on the island.

***

Three years after Paul hired me, he announced he was leaving the high school for an alternative school in downtown Everett that served adjudicated kids off the island.

I looked into the stats of the school where Paul was transferring. It was a 15-minute ferry ride across the water. The dropout rate was an astounding 70 percent. I knew Paul could rescue the school, even with stats that sank to the bottom of the ocean. If anyone could pull that school up, it would be Paul. But it would be a Herculean job.

As my third school year drew to a close, I packed up my markers, paper, collage magazines, glue, scissors, watercolors, glitter, clay and yarn. Paul came in as I packed. I was fighting back tears; it was so difficult for me to say goodbye to him. I had some trouble with attachment – but it wasn't attaching that was my problem, it was detaching.

Paul pulled up a seat at my desk where the kids usually sat and asked if I would be interested in going with him to his next school.

The new school job was only a 15-minute drive from the ferry.

A lot had changed in my life on the island in the three years since I'd met Paul. I'd come without my husband, but a year later, we reunited, and he moved up to the island. We had decided to start a family and had our twins. Our marriage would not go as planned, but I was getting used to the idea that life is always different than what we imagine.

I couldn't visualize leaving my daughters, commuting and returning to work with kids at Paul's new school. In addition to the drop-out rate, they had been convicted of crimes.

Kids who had been in detention took time to connect and attach, *if* they attached. Most had rough childhoods, often with no protection from the troubled adults in their lives.

As a teacher in LA, I spent two years in a classroom with kids whose thermostats sizzled and froze. They were hot, angry and explosive, or low, withdrawn and silent, with outbursts of crying and running in circles outside on the school field.

Now, I was in the soft tenderness of new motherhood. I smelled of milk, coffee and baby powder, with binkies in my pockets. My hair was gummed together with snack bits from baby fingers.

I hadn't thought about how I would work after the birth of my daughters. I could no longer think ahead. They filled every moment with rocking, feeding schedules, diaper changes, songs and stories, laundry piling up. And I was supposed to decide where I would work and who would watch our babies if I left the house.

Paul helped me with the decision.

"What if you just 'visit' the school for two weeks, observe and give me some ideas on programs to help the kids get more attached to the school?"

I said yes to two weeks.

I didn't want to make promises I couldn't keep, not to such a high-needs group of kids, not to Paul and his school of troublemakers.

4

A NEW SCHOOL

Everett, WA

In October, my daughters were nine months old, and I came to work at Paul's new school – for two weeks.

The cement school building couldn't help but look dirty. It was usually raining in Washington. The building was surrounded by wet streets; passing cars splashed mud onto the sidewalk and building.

It didn't look like a school. There was no field, no parking lot for teachers, no reader board announcing school events to the world. The school didn't even have a sign on the building. There was no grassy area, just a cement sidewalk in front of the glass door to the school. There was no place for a school bus to park; in fact, no school buses came to the school. The kids found their own way, walking and using free passes the teachers gave them for public buses.

The first thing I noticed was that the kids differed greatly from kids I had worked with anywhere else. These Everett kids were not like my LA kids. Yes, both groups of teens had spent time in lock-up, but all my LA kids got on a big yellow school bus at the end of each day to a home and at least one parent or guardian. The LA kids came to school showered, in clean clothes and new sneakers, and fed. I never worried that the kids in my class in LA hadn't eaten over the weekend.

Poverty was the most noticeable feature for every kid in the Everett school. They did not have shoes that fit, they seemed to not have hairbrushes or combs, and they wore ill-fitting clothes. In fact, their clothes – torn and full of holes – may have belonged to other people. In some cases, the one outfit they were wearing was all they had. They'd wear the same clothes day after day, getting dirtier and dirtier. One teacher asked if we could set up an area in the school building for showering and laundry. The kids smelled of sweat, salt, cheese and unbrushed teeth, all blending together like sour milk and garbage left too long under the sink.

These kids had no pencils, no backpacks, no books. I thought at least half of them came to school to get out of the rain, use the bathroom and get as much food as possible.

Some of these kids were beyond "neglected." Many were on their own. They were the loneliest kids I had ever met. They didn't gather the way teens do in high school, in little clumps or cliques. Each kid was their own island, quiet, aloof. I recognized their sealed silence. When I was a very young child and endured a trauma, I stopped talking for a while. Completely stopped. The suppressed voices in the school were a loud alarm bell in my head. Trauma was stalking these teens. Trauma has a presence that can be felt, coming off our skin, prickling – a charged current I felt inside my body and all around me.

Paul opened the school as early as possible. Kids slept against the wet, cold concrete walls of the building. When Paul unlocked the front door, the kids would appear like seagulls when you hold out bread. They swooped in from the alleyways, the street corners, the covered parking lot across the street.

I never saw kids so eager to get inside of a school building.

For breakfast, the kids had choices of cereal and milk in disposable paper bowls, served in the building's basement. The basement room was the largest room, and the whole student body could fit in the room at once. It wasn't an actual school cafeteria, of course. There was no stove or place to serve food. It didn't have windows. It had vinyl flooring and dreary painted walls. The room had folding chairs and some round tables, both large and small.

Lunch wasn't made on-site. It came to the school in a white van. The back doors of the van opened, and workers pulled large metal trays of food from racks and carried them into the basement. Everything was served on paper plates. The teachers would eat with the kids. Upstairs from the basement were the classrooms. The classrooms had been small offices. Walls had been removed to create classrooms. The former offices had large windows, letting in lots of natural light from the street. But as classrooms, they were not ideal; the windows were distracting, as the kids could watch comings and goings on the street all day.

Each of the five teachers had a room to set up as their own. The classrooms had blackboards, single chairs and desks, bookcases. That nothing was hanging on the walls in the halls or classrooms made everything feel impermanent. Teachers shared supplies; the overhead projector was shared from class to class, and the copy machine was in the basement. None of the classrooms had closets, so the teachers had to find places to put supplies they didn't want stolen. There were two empty rooms that were too small for classrooms. Each one had just a single round table that could seat four people. No windows. I had my choice of the small rooms to see kids.

My two-week commitment came and went.

I continued showing up a few mornings each week. Paul extended my contract each month, agreeing to be very flexible about my hours, never more than a few mornings each week. I couldn't walk away from the school and the neediness I saw all around me.

My mothering instincts were on fire from caring for my daughters. Mothering sharpened my senses.

Clarence, Ivy and Emanuel were three of the kids I worked with on the mornings they made it to school. Like all the kids in this school, they were years behind their peers academically.

Ivy had the typical features of a child with Fetal Alcohol Syndrome. Her skin was pale white; white-blond curls hung just below her ears. She was confused when given a set of instructions in the classroom. I broke down tasks to make them doable for her. She lived with her aunt and uncle, sometimes. Other times, she was wandering the streets of Everett, looking for her mom in the motels on the rundown side of town. Ivy often wore the same cream-colored, short-sleeved sweater with pearls on it and plaid tweed bell bottoms. I'm certain she found these clothes buried in her aunt's closet. They were decades out of fashion, but the softness of the sweater and delicacy of the pearls fit Ivy's gentle manner. I don't think Ivy had a single thing that belonged to her. Her shoes were way too big and flopped on her feet. She pined for her missing mom. The only way I could get Ivy to focus on school was to give her some time to first talk about her mom. Had she seen her the day before, wandering the streets drunk? Would she like to write a note to her? Getting to start her day talking about her mom would help her move on to other subjects. Without this first contact, she was staring out the window of school, dazed-looking and lost.

I grouped her with Clarence.

Clarence was a follower. Whatever trouble he had been in, whatever got him into juvenile detention, I was certain someone else had led the way. He was a large, overweight kid with dark brown hair, easy to spot in a crowd or a line-up. He came to school in a white T-shirt and the same jeans every day. No jacket, no hat, no socks. Just a T-shirt, no matter how cold it was outside. Clarence said he lived with his cousins. I could never puzzle through how he was related to his "cousins," leading me to think he was living with a gang. Clarence came to school because he was court-ordered to do so. All the kids at our school were court-ordered to be there. Their probation officers were down the hall in the same building. If you missed school, your probation officer knew in five minutes, because the probation officers had a secretary pick up our attendance log at 9:15am every day.

I started the day with Clarence by trying to separate him from his friends. If I didn't succeed, he wouldn't think for himself. In my morning group with Ivy and Emanuel, Clarence wouldn't have anyone to feed him answers or interrupt him every time he talked.

Emanuel didn't talk. He could talk, but it was rare if he spoke a word. I hoped that this safe little morning group would create an opening into his world of silence. I started the day with something simple for Emanuel: a game of hangman. He didn't offer any words, just a single letter. He seemed to enjoy playing with Ivy and Clarence. Ivy could never guess the word. It gave Clarence a chance to think for himself. Emanuel was smart, and I could see that he got the words easily, but would let Clarence and Ivy stumble their way through.

I had a hard time believing these three deserved to be locked up in juvenile detention. All three were wounded, withdrawn, soft kids. They had unbearably hard lives. Emanuel was raised by his dad, and his dad was deployed in the military. Emanuel said he lived "here and there."

If they made it to school, these three were at the school early: Ivy in her plaid bell bottoms, Clarence often soaking wet from rain and Emanuel silent in a sweatshirt with the hood up. But some days, one or two of them were absent. I didn't know if they would ever return, thinking of the dropout rate. But then, my morning trio would surprise me and show up.

***

As I listened to the stories from each of the kids in this school, I realized they had another thing in common, aside from having been in detention: Many did not have homes. They had couches they crashed on, relatives that "took them in," but the key word was "sometimes."

Almost none of the kids had a bedroom, a family, meals they could count on, a stable home.

This was my first time working with kids who were "homeless." I had worked with kids labeled "aggressive," "violent," "emotionally disturbed," "sexually provocative" and "dangerous." But never "homeless."

It was like a kid was living nowhere, suspended in midair. They didn't know where to go when school let out. They didn't know which way to go on the street as it got dark. They had to find a place to be until the morning when the school opened. They had no place. No home.

It's an enormous thing not to have. If you don't have a home, you also don't have food, parents taking care of you, clothes, a bathroom, a toothbrush, running water – the safety that comes with parents, caring and shelter.

My job at the school was to help Paul and the teachers reverse the dropout rate. How could we help the kids stick to school? We couldn't be only teachers or a principal or school counselor.

We couldn't be offering a school, and only a school. For so many, we had to be their home.

Holli's place was on the floor, under my desk. But she couldn't live under my damn desk. Nothing in my training or education had prepared me for working with kids who didn't have homes. I didn't have any reference points for this, except one.

There was a younger part of me who was watching all of this in horror. She was responsible for everything. She was asking, "What kind of mother are you? What kind of mother would leave all these kids with no place to go?"

I thought of the book I read to my daughters, though they were still too young to understand *The Runaway Bunny*. If the bunny becomes a fish, the mother bunny becomes a fisherman. If the bunny becomes a rock on a mountain, the mother bunny becomes a mountain climber.

I didn't know how to ignore the problem that the kids did not have homes. The responsible-for-everything child inside me and the mother, who had to prove she would not abandon her children, joined forces. It was not just that I would never abandon my own babies; I would not abandon other children either. I stayed on at the school, beyond my two weeks, because I couldn't turn away from the neediest kids I had ever seen.

5

FIO

When it came time to give my recommendations to Paul on how
to reduce the dropout rate, I wasn't able to think of a curriculum
the school could offer that would help. Arts, food, small classes and
caring teachers – the school already had those things, and it wasn't
a substitute for having a place to sleep at night. When school let
out each day, half the kids had nowhere to go. Holli was sleeping
under my desk because it was the only place where she felt she could
safely close her eyes. Holli and too many of the other kids would be
awake out on the streets at night and return to the school building
exhausted and hungry in the morning.

I gave Paul my one and only recommendation: "Shelter is the
only answer."

"Great idea. Figure out what it would take to make that happen."
Paul was big on the FIO ("Figure It Out") approach.

Paul knew how to push my buttons. FIO was my favorite approach
to anything. There is freedom in FIO. You aren't bound by anyone's
idea of anything. It's all about creativity, trying things, testing ideas
and making discoveries.

Paul, as my boss, was blessing the mission.

I started by approaching the most obvious place: the school district.
They were invested in changing the dropout rate at this school.
I thought the school district had the best capacity to support the kids.
They had lots of buildings that weren't occupied at night, they had
gyms with showers, and they knew how to hire good people. I even
had ideas about where the school district could put the shelter.

"You could open a teen shelter next door to our school."
I reasoned they had already converted an office building into a school; they could take another building and make a shelter.

The superintendent nodded and patiently explained to me that shelter was too far outside what school districts did. "We're not in the housing business; we're in the education business. Go to the housing programs." He assured me he would partner with any shelter that stepped up to solve the problem. I left our meeting with nothing.

I returned to calling the list of housing programs in the phone book. This time, instead of asking them to shelter teens, I offered to help them. My offer was very specific.

"What if I volunteer to help your organization for two years to create a housing program for teens? You don't have to pay me."

I wanted to convey to the housing programs that I wasn't trying to create a paying job for myself. I had a job and career. But the housing program directors knew I didn't have any experience setting up a shelter. I didn't have any idea about codes, getting permits, safety issues, staffing or the typical problems one faces in operating a shelter day to day. In their wisdom, not a single housing program took me up on the offer. These phone calls made me the laughingstock of the housing community.

Without a single housing program willing to consider a teen shelter, I turned to the Division of Children and Family Services. First, I did some homework, reading state codes late at night trying to understand why the state didn't have housing for kids living on the street. I was trying to learn as much as I could about the state codes, deciphering bureaucratic doublespeak.

On the day that I met with two administrators at the Division of Children and Family Services, which was housed in an eight-story building, I didn't have childcare. Without a thought about my professional appearance, driven by the necessity of seeing what we could work out, I brought my twin babies. Their stroller barely fit in the elevator to the top floor.

A man and a woman were there to meet me. As I talked, I took turns lifting each of my babies onto my lap and bouncing them on my leg. The woman was in charge. She eyed me as if she were well-trained in the bureaucratic art of "letting the other person do all the talking." Her face gave nothing away. The man dutifully made notes and said little. However, I learned two things.

One, they didn't take kids from the street to services. It was their job to remove kids from "dangerous families." These kids weren't living with families. Because the kids weren't living with their families, they couldn't be removed from them. They didn't meet the "dangerous family" criteria. There was no family, thus no danger.

I couldn't follow their logic. Questions I asked did not make it any clearer. We moved on to point number two: Families were not volunteering to foster teenagers. There were so few placements for teens in foster care because this age group is tough when they've been abused and tortured most of their lives. They don't follow rules, have outbursts of anger and are incommunicative, especially when handed to new families. If the Division of Child and Family Services did take a teenager, there wasn't anywhere to put them.

I left this meeting in tears, trying to fit my twin stroller into the cramped elevator. The words they'd said had stuck into my flesh and started eating their way inward, to my childhood.

Just hearing the words "remove" and "dangerous family" brought up things I'd tried to keep pushed down.

I didn't talk about my childhood. No one in my new home in the Pacific Northwest – not Paul, not anyone – knew where I was from.

This conversation about "dangerous families" ripped open old wounds. Wounds I couldn't do anything about. It all happened so long ago.

I refocused my attention on my daughters, taking them for a walk in their stroller. I could feel the cool Northwest air on my skin and took turns snuggling each of my girls against my chest. I could feel their heartbeats. It was a comfort.

Next, I met with our county's Children's Commission. They gave me ten minutes on their agenda to describe our school's kids' need for shelter. The Children's Commission met around the corner from the school. I discovered this group cared about homeless youth. They cared about all kinds of issues. The Children's Commission was tackling a smorgasbord that included literacy, shortening detention stays, drug problems spreading to younger kids, too few foster placements, and preventing child abuse and sexual assault of minors, sex trafficking of children and suicide. As for the teens who were homeless, they'd applied for a federal grant to start a teen shelter, but they had been rejected for the last few years. They told me they would continue to apply every year; they weren't giving up.

I returned to Paul. I had no faith that waiting for federal grants to fall from the sky would help the kids in our school. I regurgitated my meetings and phone calls, listing all the people I'd met along the way.

Paul sat on his desk, his large feet touching the floor like he was in a chair, his hands clasped together in his lap, his head nodding, listening and not interrupting. He was not rushing to go somewhere else. I mapped every step of my search for him. I'd gone begging to the housing programs, the state, the school district, and still I had nothing.

Paul said, "There is only one final option."

I shook my head. He didn't get it. "No, I tried everything."

He pointed his finger at me and said, "You could open a shelter yourself."

"Huh?" My mouth hung open. My mind was vacant.

Paul's response was, "Figure it out."

Paul tutored me on what he knew about nonprofits. The thought of opening a shelter by myself would never have occurred to me. But all you needed to be a nonprofit was to file a piece of paper with the State of Washington. Getting a driver's license was far more complicated than forming a nonprofit organization. The only thing required for creating a nonprofit organization was three names on a piece of paper. The paper is called "Articles of Incorporation." On the Articles of Incorporation, I needed a name for the organization. I wrote "Cocoon House" in the blank.

As for the three names on the articles of incorporation, Paul was named board president. I was the executive director. We needed one more name. I dashed over to the probation side of the building. I poked my head in Steve's office. Steve was the probation officer I spent the most time checking in with about kids. We were always in and out of each other's offices. He was experienced, and he checked on more than just kids' attendance – I had the sense he cared about them. He was on the phone and waved his arm for me to start talking.

"Hey Steve, can you be listed on the paperwork as the secretary for our new nonprofit?"

Steve nodded yes.

An hour later Steve poked his head in my office. "What's that nonprofit for?"

"We're going to open a teen shelter."

He bent his head down, chin to chest, peering over his glasses.

"Good luck with that!" He pressed his hand flat on my doorjamb and then walked away laughing.

There was no way any of us could have imagined a teen shelter. All I could see was the Articles of Incorporation – it was a piece of paper and a check for the filing fee.

I was living one week at a time as a mommy; my plans did not extend beyond the promises of morning childcare. All of my afternoons and evenings were full, singing Raffi songs; reading *Grandfather Twilight*; changing diapers; rocking my daughters in my lap; reciting *The Owl and The Pussycat*; holding one of my soft-haired daughters against my chest until it was her sister's turn for some snuggling; mashing and testing foods to figure out which ones did not cause constipation; going to the park; hosting Friday morning baby play group with other moms and babies.

My daughters were a year old. I was being remade by my precious babies, motherhood, Mother Nature and my maternal instincts. My whole being was re-forming. I was very happy as a mom and part-time psychotherapist. That was more than enough. For God's sake, I was not aspiring to lead or run an organization. I was not sitting around bored with free time and wondering what else I could take on.

Though I believed the kids and the town needed a teen shelter, I was not interested in becoming a nonprofit director. I didn't know what was involved, but whatever it was, it wasn't a goal of mine to run a nonprofit. For some, that is their goal or dream job.

I'd met people who ran nonprofit organizations. They were experienced working in nonprofits, steeped in a particular issue. Many went to school to be social workers, public administrators, social entrepreneurs, environmentalists, public health workers. That was not me.

In my mind, I told myself I was taking a quick detour on my path in life: "Solve the problem right in front of you. Try to get a teen shelter open and then hand it off to a housing agency." That was the extent of the entire plan. I estimated it would take two years.

I knew nothing about what it would take.

6

WHERE SHOULD I SEND YOU?

Memories, New York
1965

The night after meeting with the administrators at the Division of Children and Family Services, my daughters were in their cribs, sucking their thumbs, yellow blankets and stuffed toys surrounding them, owls calling outside. I felt peace descending. As I walked out to my kitchen for tea, my chest ached for Holli, wherever she was. She had stopped attending school.

She was on the dropout list.

And Holli wasn't the only one. I thought of all the people I met who wouldn't help with the teen shelter idea. They were also dropouts. Dropping out of solving the problem. Sure, I could give them credit for all the other problems they addressed, but when it came to helping kids that were homeless, they offered nothing.

I carried my tea to bed and crawled in beside my husband. Socrates stretched out over my legs; floral wallpaper with a dark blue background surrounded us. I listened for Somer and Aliza's synchronized breathing. Asleep. Moonlight was coming through the window. I heard the raccoon scratching at the leftover dog kibbles in the bottom of Socrates's bowl on the porch.

I held a book open as if I were reading. But I wasn't reading. I wasn't in the bed at all. I was floating, drifting with the little girl I carried inside. Words grinding in my mind: "removing children from dangerous families."

I thought of all the problems I witnessed in my family as a child, all the issues I'd excavated in grad school – the paranoia, the delusions, mania, law-breaking, addiction, violence, abandonment and inability to parent. I had never summed it all up as a dangerous family.

But the dangers were persistent as rain.

***

When I was a little girl, I had a mother, a father and a baby brother. The family I started out with was whole. We lived together in a house, in a neighborhood. Surrounding our little family was an extended family: two sets of grandparents and six cousins. Three cousins from my mother's side and three cousins from my father's side. The eight of us cousins were all close in age. My cousins were like parts of my body. Their homes were my homes too. I slept in their bunk beds, rolled in the piles of leaves we gathered in the fall, dragged sleds up and down the snow-covered hills of their neighborhoods and danced in sprinklers with them in summer. I had no awareness of being separate from them. We were a family.

My mother was an artist who liked to draw, paint and sew. She put on makeup and took time dressing, taking clothes off and putting them on, off and on, off and on. Discarded clothes were everywhere. She made messes and never cleaned up: spilled paint, spilled drinks. There was always a trail of broken things that led to my mother.

My mother was untamed. She could go from a high-pitched, sweet sound like she was talking to a pet, to yelling, throwing things and speaking incoherently in minutes. In an old home movie of me as a toddler, I am running in fear from my mother.

Once she was driving 90 miles per hour while my baby brother and I sloshed around in the backseat. She careened around corners until a cop pulled us over. The cop kept repeating "90 miles an hour" like there was something very wrong. Cops followed my mother like an entourage. Her being pulled over, searched and locked up, needing bail, were as normal as going to the beauty parlor for other moms. My mom was always in trouble with the law. Someone needed to respond to her constant crisis; it was often the police.

My father liked games: bowling, tennis, golf and cards. We went to the harbor on Sundays to feed the ducks and then go bowling. My earliest memory is of my dad teaching me to "Twist and Shout." I could see him tilting sideways, laughing, spitting his drink into the air, clapping for me to keep twisting, all while ashes from his cigarette dropped to the floor. My father tilted sideways from being too drunk to stand up straight.

Music played day and night in our house. I ate TV dinners on a folding snack table alone, while watching the Mouseketeers. We had two Black housekeepers that took care of my brother and me. These two young women were the first in a long line of Black women who raised us, none ever staying more than a few months. The time between goodbyes to each caring and attentive "housekeeper" became shorter and shorter. But they each provided the constant attention and care one needs to give small children. Eventually, I realized their departures were inevitable.

There were houses next door to our house. I played outside with the neighbor kids. I went to nursery school on a bus that picked me up from home. Every night my dad put me to bed, making puppet shows for me and my pet turtle. My mother would sometimes sit in the chair across from my bed and draw. Long after I was in bed under my pink princess blanket, the music kept playing.

Night after night, the party went on while I slept. My parents' friends came and went – smoking, dancing, laughing – until everyone fell asleep on the living room floor.

Then my life changed. I was four years old.

***

One night, as the house became quiet and the music stopped, I often slipped from my bed at night to tiptoe around the sleeping friends on the floor. I probably collected some interesting things, picking up the empty glasses and tasting the juice at the bottom. I may have counted the cigarettes in the ashtrays and made sure they weren't smoking.

I looked up at the sudden arrival of blue flashing lights outside. Someone was banging at the door and yelling. I may have been running down the hall to my parents' bedroom. A police officer grabbed me, wrapped me in a towel and carried me out of the house. The police officer passed me to my mother's father, Poppy, who was standing outside on the street.

My grandfather watched the house as the raid continued, gripping me tightly. The blue lights hurt my eyes. In the whirling blue, my mother was screaming, and I heard smashing sounds like thunder from inside the house. As the blue lights became a storm, police dragged my father on the ground out of the house, handcuffed. I screamed for my dad. I was kicking my grandfather to free myself so I could get my baby brother. Then, the police carried my little brother out. My grandfather put my baby brother and me in the back seat of his car and drove away from the sirens and screams.

Where were we going?

We drove to Poppy and Gram's pink house. Poppy said we would live with them in their pink house until we went to "court." I did not understand what court was.

I continued going to nursery school. A new Black housekeeper, Margaret, was hired at Poppy and Gram's house to watch over me and my brother. Margaret rocked my brother on her lap, which I found reassuring.

Eventually, the day came when I went to court. I don't know how many times I went to court, I only remember the final time I went.

***

"Court" was the biggest building I had ever seen. I walked down a long hallway where my shoes tapped and echoed with each step. I walked and walked down a long hall, holding hands with my Poppy until we came to large doors.

"Stop there. That's our stop," boomed his dark voice.

I stood in front of the closed doors. My stomach squeezed when my mother appeared in the long hallway walking toward me.

But my Grammy took hold of my hand. Grammy was small, almost child-size in height. She wore smocks at home, but when we went out, like now, she wore a skirt to her knees, panty hose, brown shoes, a blouse and sweater, topped off by many jangling necklaces and gold bracelets. Grammy, who always said she could see the future, grabbed my hand. Her hand was my anchor. My mother walked past me. She walked past me like I wasn't there, like she didn't see me.

"Hello, Linda," Grammy said. Her daughter ignored her. My mother opened the door and went into the courtroom without saying a word.

Poppy held the door, and Gram and I went in the big room with long wooden benches. There were other people in the room.

Grammy tugged my arm hard, pulled me to her like I was on a leash, and said, "Remember what I told you."

She put her finger to her lips.

That was her way of telling me to lie or keep her secrets.

While I already knew Grammy had many secrets, I had no idea how many secrets and lies would lay ahead in my life with her.

We walked past the benches to the front row. I slid in next to Poppy. I turned my head to see who was in the room.

"DADDY!" I wanted to run to him.

Grammy blocked my exit from the row.

Daddy waved, blew a kiss and winked at me. I tried to wink back.

My father's sister Shirley, her husband Stu and my father's parents were all in the courtroom. But something was wrong with my family. No one was acting like they usually did.

I knew everyone. But I was the only kid. Where were my cousins?

Then the wall moved!

"How did the wall move?" I asked Gram. She didn't answer me.

A gray-haired white man came in. He wore a big black coat that went all the way to the floor and over his shoes.

We all stood up.

He called my name.

"How did he know my name?" I tugged on Gram's bracelet. She looked at me and said, "Just do what he says."

"But why?" She didn't answer.

The man in the long black coat asked me to walk up to a box with a chair and sit in it.

He told someone to get phone books for me to sit on so I could see above the box.

I sat on two phone books, and they kept sliding underneath me.

"Whoa, that was fun," I thought, slipping back and forth.

The man in the black coat then asked me to go behind the wall with him.

"What's behind the wall?" I asked.

"My office. I want to show it to you."

I went with him behind the wall. He closed the door-wall. He had a desk and a chair in his office.

He sat down at the desk. He asked if I wanted to draw and gave me paper and a pencil.

I told him I wanted to use a typewriter. My Poppy had an office where I could use a typewriter.

The man said he didn't have a typewriter.

"Can I ask you some questions?"

"Sure! Can I ask you some questions?"

"Yes, go ahead, ask yours first."

"Why are you wearing a big black coat?"

"It's my robe. I am a judge, and this is what I wear in my court. Now, I get a turn. Can I ask you a question?"

I nodded.

"Who do you want to live with?"

"Do you mean me and my brother? I have a baby brother. He's mine. He goes where I go."

"Yes. I'm sorry. I mean, who should I send you and your baby brother to live with? Draw me a picture of who you want to live with."

"We can go anywhere?"

"Yes, if you could go anywhere to live with your baby brother, where would that be?"

Grammy had told me someone would ask me this question.

I looked around the room. Grammy and Poppy could not hear me in this room. The door was closed.

I drew my picture and gave it to the Judge. I was certain I had found the very best place for my baby brother and me.

"Who is that?" he asked.

"That is Santa Claus. I want us to live in the North Pole with Santa Claus."

In a rather long and confusing conversation, the judge told me we would not be going to live with Santa Claus.

He told me I would return to the courtroom, sit on the phone books, look over at my family in the courtroom and tell him who I wanted to live with. I could only pick one person. My mommy and daddy were not choices.

But they were in the room, watching me choose.

No one in the court knew the big secret I had been told by Grammy. Grammy and Poppy told me that if I picked them in the court, I would get to keep my baby brother. They told me if I picked anyone else, Adam would be sent away, and I would never see him again.

I looked around the courtroom and saw my family.

The judge had me sit on the phone books in the booth and say aloud that I chose to live with Gram and Poppy.

The judge explained I was not going to the North Pole, but I would be going back to the pink house with my brother.

But instead of going to the pink house, Poppy drove us to an apartment I had never seen. My mother, who I hadn't seen in months, other than in court, was inside. My grandfather carried my brother to a crib inside. I begged him and Grammy not to leave us there. He pulled the door closed and left us on the other side of the door with my mother, in an apartment in New York City. I had no idea how to find our way back to the pink house from there.

***

I don't know how many weeks or months we lasted. One day a police officer saw me walking alone in the streets of New York City after kindergarten let out. My mother did not show up at school to walk me back to the apartment. I set off walking on my own. The police officer walked with me all the way to the door of the apartment. My mother was using her pretend voice with the police officer. She was slurring her words and was partially dressed. The police officer came into the apartment, walked around, met my baby brother and then left.

My mother screamed her head off at me for bringing a "pig" home. I can't remember all that happened after. But when she took her cigarettes and left the apartment, I dialed the phone number taped to the table by the telephone, following each number written on the paper. Gram answered the phone. I told her she had to come pick us up. I hung up and got a washcloth to hold on my bleeding head.

My grandparents came that night in their car. I remember it was dark outside when we left the apartment. My brother was sleeping on my lap in the back of their car. I watched the lights of the city go by. We drove to their pink house.

***

My parents had visitation rights.

Birthdays, holidays, school plays, being home sick with fevers, graduations, all went by unnoticed by my parents. I became a half-child – part of me was missing without my parents. When my father visited the pink house, less than five times in 14 years, I grew fearful of him. As years went by, I no longer belonged to him.

My mother visited the pink house when she needed money from Gram and Poppy. She would throw a tantrum in the pink house until she got the money she came for, and then disappear in a taxi.

Being separated from my "unfit" parents was a loss for me. They were my parents and my family for the first four years of my life. Then they broke apart and evaporated – gone. The separation from my cousins and other grandparents was another unbearable thing.

There is only one thing that I remember from going to court, and it was talking to the judge. In the 1960s, though I was between ages four and five, I was testifying in court against my parents. I did not understand that I was testifying. (This is something my father later explained to me in therapy when I was in my 20s.) As a small child, I was interviewed by a psychiatrist, a doctor, lawyers and a judge. The only one I remember is the judge and the final day in court.

I remembered it, and for years and years after, this scene replayed every single night when I laid down to sleep. It was like watching a movie that I couldn't make stop replaying.

My grandparents hated my father and blamed him for my mother's problems, so Adam and I were completely shut off from our cousins on his side of the family. And when my mother's sister visited, she no longer had her children. My three cousins, her children, were also suddenly missing. Their pictures remained on the wall in the pink house, but no one ever said what had happened to them. I don't remember if I was told they'd died, but I somehow came to believe they'd died in a car accident. Another devastating loss.

Losing everyone left me with a fear of losing things. I also had a fear of being left. It wasn't a phobia – an unrealistic fear – because it wasn't just an idea in my head. It was reality – an experience. After being left in New York City, I didn't trust my grandparents. I slept with Gram in her bed until I was 11, to keep an eye on her. I was terrified every night that I would go to sleep and wake up to find her and Poppy gone.

Like a tree that grows around a lightning strike, I grew up with this scar of abandonment inside me.

***

Now, facing conversations about the teen shelter, about kids having nowhere safe to go, I was standing in the ruins of that shattered place. Abandonment and losing everything were not just words to me. I felt the little four-year-old girl inside of me still trying to answer the judge's question, "Where should I send you?" Except now she had to answer when she looked at other kids: "Where should I send you?"

I was determined to keep searching.

I felt the little girl inside me, listening to every conversation I had with shelters, the superintendent, the people who "removed children from dangerous families." The responsible-for-everything child carried the weight of the world on her tiny shoulders. She was searching for shelter.

7

BINGO

Everett, WA

After I filed our Articles of Incorporation with Washington State, Cocoon House was officially a nonprofit organization. Paul explained that I could now go out and raise money.

I had never raised money or asked anyone for donations. As a child, I was not a Girl Scout and missed out on all the lessons on cookie sales. I remembered the little brown dresses many of the girls wore to our school and not being a member of their club.

I remembered the bright orange UNICEF boxes, too. In elementary school, they gave us flat cardboard pieces that we folded into boxes. Then, when we went out trick-or-treating at Halloween, my brother, my best friend Bonnie and I each carried the little orange boxes door to door and got them filled with pennies. The pennies went to the United Nations International Children's Emergency Fund (UNICEF). UNICEF was created in 1946, its website says, "at the end of the Second World War, when a refugee crisis emerged unlike any the world had seen. Many children were orphaned by the war; the money benefited any children in need without discrimination." This was the only experience I had fundraising.

I needed more than a box of pennies to open a teen shelter. But there were some lessons in the UNICEF boxes that did come in handy.

I wasn't sure where I should begin. Paul mentioned that service clubs give out money. I had no connection to a service club. I opened the phone book and read a list of service clubs in the Yellow Pages. (This was before the internet.)

Seeing a long list of service clubs, I felt hopeful. I phoned to ask them how to apply to for money.

The North Everett Lions Club was the first service group at which someone answered the phone – no answering machine.

The guy who answered the phone said, "One of our speakers canceled tonight. There's a 15-minute spot for a speaker. Come on down to the bingo parlor on Oakes Avenue."

"How will I know it is a bingo parlor?" I asked.

He laughed and said, "Look for the blue door. You can't miss it. It says B-I-N-G-O on top of the building. You got that?" As he spelled out "bingo" slowly, I felt like an idiot.

"Yes. I'll be there, 7pm."

I had my first speaking gig to raise money. I drove to Macy's to buy a clean white blouse to wear with my black pants. I didn't know what people wore to bingo halls. I wanted to give it my best. At 6:30pm, I found the blue door. I knocked. No one heard me. I could hear lots of noise inside. I banged my hand on the door. No one responded. I kicked the door.

A white-haired older man walked up behind me and said, "Have you tried pulling the knob?"

He yanked on the doorknob and held the door for me.

I entered a smoky room with wood paneling on one side and blue paint on the other three walls. One wall had a glass window where I could see into another room where people were playing bingo, seated at rows of long tables. Someone at the front of the room was spinning a silver metal cage and pulling out numbers.

In the room with paneling where I stood, there wasn't any bingo. This room had a buffet and seating for about 40 people.

"Miss, can I help you?" a different white-haired man asked.

"I'm your speaker for tonight."

"Well, you don't look like a Seth or John."

I gave him my name and explained I was filling in because someone had canceled.

White-haired men lined up at the buffet table. White-haired men sat at rectangular tables.

One of them grabbed my hand.

"Hey, missy, can you get me another roll?" That's when I realized I was dressed like the two catering servers.

"Sure."

I grabbed a roll for him. I asked if he knew where the speaker should sit. The doorknob guy overheard me and pointed to chairs and a table at the front of the room on a stage.

I took a seat alone on the stage. Someone offered me dinner. I thought it would be rude to say no, but my stomach was jumping too much to eat. One guy stepped up to the table to sit at the other end, and another guest speaker came in. He was in a shirt and tie. He introduced himself to me as Seth and took some paper from his briefcase. He had a speech. I sank in my chair, feeling small and unprepared.

I had nothing. I asked him for a pen and started writing out what I planned to say on my napkin.

As the old Lions men ate dinner, I wondered why there were no women in their club. I felt like I was the wrong gender to be making a request of the group.

When it was my turn to speak, an older gentleman introduced me. "Missy, what's your name?"

He then looked out at the Lions eating dinner and added, "She's here because John couldn't make it. She has an idea to tell us about. Something to do with kids. Let's give her a warm Lions welcome."

I walked to the podium with my napkin. My hands had soaked the ink with sweat, and the ink smeared onto my hands. Undeterred, I explained how I started a nonprofit last week and needed to buy a shelter. The tag in my new blouse itched, making me scratch my neck. I asked the Lions if they could chip in $10,000 for the new shelter for teens. I would then go to each service club listed in the phone book – the Rotary, Soroptimists, Kiwanis and the rest – and ask each of them for $10,000 so I'd have enough to start the shelter. Now and then, I was interrupted with bingo calls and whoops from the game going on in the next room.

All the men stopped eating and became quiet.

"B-13," echoed in the silence.

The white-haired white men looked at me, blinking. I wondered if they understood what I said. I was telling the men about a shelter for teens, a place that didn't exist. I was asking them to help me create something that didn't exist for kids who were sleeping under bridges, in unlocked cars or in parking garages.

Then the questions came: "How will you fund it?" "Who will staff it?" "What's the operating budget?" "Who else has given money?"

I remembered being in third grade. I was standing in front of the class in a white shirt and a blue dress. I was giving a book report — only I hadn't finished the book and didn't know how it ended. Gary raised his hand and asked, "How did it end?" I didn't know. I didn't finish the book. When you are in third grade and give a book report, you are required to read the book. I made up the ending to the book. I lied. But making up the ending was a terrible idea. A girl in my class raised her hand and called me a liar. She had read the book and told the class how it ended.

As the Lions asked me questions, I knew I did not have any answers. There wasn't a single question that I knew the answer to. And the white-haired men seemed to know either a lot about running a shelter or a lot about things I didn't know. The lessons from my third-grade book report were still stinging. I would not lie.

Two younger men slipped into the back of the room. Both were apparently lawyers and started asking me legal questions. The three best answers I could give to all the questions was, "I don't know," "I'll figure it out," and, "That's a good question."

After I failed to answer a single question, the elder man who introduced me stood up as a signal my time was up. I thanked them for listening and walked past their tables and chairs to leave. As my hand touched the doorknob, the next speaker for the night, Seth in the tie, stood up.

"She's right," he said. "There are kids in this town that need a shelter. We all see them on the streets every day. And yet they are invisible." Seth, I learned, was the beloved son of the town, the prosecutor. They elected him three times. All the Lions knew him.

I thanked Seth and slipped out the door.

The next day, I shared my embarrassing performance with Paul.

As the morning went on, while I met with my kids in the basement classroom, I got pink slips of paper with phone messages written on them slipped under my office door. Each message from the office said the same thing: "The Lions called."

For my next two days at work, pink slips were piling up under the door of my office.

After three days of fake messages from the Lions, I went to Paul's office. I waved the pink slips in the air, "Enough! I need no more reminders about that night."

Paul looked up with an eager smile. "What did they want?"

"Don't be ridiculous. I didn't call these fake numbers." I shook my head at this latest prank.

He pushed the phone in front of me and shouted, "For God's sake, CALL THEM BACK! The calls were real."

"Paul, please." I didn't believe him. I expected to dial and hear someone laughing at me on the other end.

But he insisted. It would, at least, put an end to the joke. So, I dialed the number. A guy answered.

"You are tough to get ahold of." He explained he was a lawyer in the Lions Club.

"That was a terrible idea you proposed to us. We have a much better one. Come down to my office. I'm just up the street from the school you work at. I'm Bob."

I looked at Paul after I hung up. "Some guy named Bob wants to see me."

I held up a paper with his full name written on it.

Paul nodded. "Impressive; he owns the local baseball team."

"Come with me to meet him." I thought maybe Paul would be better at fielding questions.

Paul put his arm on my shoulder. "This is all yours. You earned this; take the bat and swing."

I got in my car, drove up Broadway and parked outside a one-story building. There were two attorneys listed on the door. A secretary extended her arm when I gave my name. She told me to just walk into the office across from her desk. I opened the door to a small office and found a guy behind a large desk and another guy in a chair near a bookcase. The bookcase held trophies. The walls had plaques, pictures of teams and awards. Every bit of wall space had honors, thank-you notes and baseballs in glass boxes. Bob was a trusted and beloved community member.

I took the empty seat.

I recognized the guys from the back of the room at the Lions Club. They'd stood out in the room of white-haired men because they were younger; Bob had brown hair, and Tom was blond.

Bob and Tom explained the Lions Club had a much better idea and an offer for me. They would like to buy a house to use as a shelter for kids.

"Go shopping. Pick out any house you want, and we'll help you through all the legal hurdles. "

The Lions were taking proceeds from their bingo parlor to buy a house. I just sat there, listening to them explain what a brilliant investment this was and how I'd help so many kids.

This was far more than I'd asked them for. A house was ten times what I had asked for. But instead of jumping for joy, my pragmatic side spoke up.

"Why would you take such a risk with me?"

The Lions didn't know me. I was working in the basement of a school up the street. "I couldn't answer a single question. Why would you do this?"

"This is zero risk for us," Tom said, like that explained everything.

"What does that mean?"

"It means we own a house. If you succeed, lots of kids will be helped. If you fail, we have all our money invested in the house. We can sell it and get our money back. We are risking nothing." Bob paused and added, "We also do think you will pull this off. You have guts."

I repeated their offer. "You want me to go out and find a house, any house in Everett, and you'll pay for it with bingo money?" They nodded yes.

Bewildered, I shook their hands. There were no papers signed.

I left that meeting with something more valuable than a house. I had partners.

8

TIMING

Whidbey Island

I returned home to Whidbey Island, to my daughters in their periwinkle-and-yellow nursery, with their matching soft, butter-colored blankets. I laid on the floor by their cribs with Socrates and our gray angora rabbit, who followed Socrates everywhere. I listened to Somer and Aliza breathing as they napped.

I couldn't imagine how I suddenly had a shelter on my hands. I was not yet 30 years old. I was terrified. It was like having a giraffe dropped off in my living room. How would I feed it, where would it live? How would I keep it alive? I didn't know how to care for a giraffe, and I didn't know how to run a youth shelter.

Lying on the floor in my daughters' nursery, I felt like I was spinning on an iron playground merry-go-round. When I was a kid, a few of us would stay off the merry-go-round, grabbing one of its metal bars and running, pulling it around as fast as we could. Then we'd jump on as it spun. The spinning would make me dizzy and nauseous.

When the Lions said they would buy a house, everything in my life was spinning.

But I said yes. I did not know what a fledgling nonprofit needed. But I knew it was the only chance to get a youth shelter open. I couldn't throw away the teens' only chance and turn down the Lions Club and their bingo money.

There is a moment when a merry-go-round is whirling, and you feel a flutter to lift yourself up and jump on. Get the timing right, or it drags your body in the dirt. This was the timing for the youth shelter. I had to jump.

But where would I find time to do this?

Curled up with my dog, I was comforted by the nursery – filled with lavender sheets, lilac blankets covered in bubbles, periwinkle bolsters around the cribs and butter-colored walls. My laughing babies would strip their beds every morning, throwing stuffed toys, blankets and bolsters into an enormous pile on the floor when they woke up, giggling, mayhem, stuffed toys flying, raucous squealing, shrieks and laughter. There was no fear in the nursery.

I had so much to learn about my daughters. What was their new favorite food this week from their little glass-jar baby-food collection? What song would they sing back to me? Which toys did they want in their bath? Every little utterance, new movement, revealed a clue about who they were, their own personalities shining through. Aliza was inciting, the one who egged her sister on to throw everything from the cribs. Somer was observant, quiet, often laughing at something her sister did, and she rarely cried. We were wrapped around each other like the moss-covered branches of the tree hugging the window of their nursery. How would a youth shelter fit into our life? None of the first-time mothering books described how to open a youth shelter.

I looked at the gray-colored diaper-changing bureau that my father and I had painted together, tiny yellow butterflies going up the side of it.

My father and I had worked hard to repair our broken bond. I was an adult when he returned to my life. He was a first-time grandfather and a getting a second chance with me. He was clean and sober, consistent, devoted to spending months at a time on Whidbey Island in a summer rental to make up for lost years, to weave his way into my heart, to have his grandchildren call him Pop-pop. He was getting it right.

Grammy and Poppy, who raised me and Adam, had loved us with a fierce and jealous love. They particularly resented our father and his sister Shirley, who, with her husband Stuart, had tried to get custody of us when our parents were declared unfit. Our maternal grandparents' love divided us from our father's side of the family for many years.

As we were growing up, Adam and I were inseparable, and I tried hard to protect him in every way I could. Once we left the pink house, though, his coping mechanisms were so different from mine that we had to take divergent paths for a while. But we always served as witnesses for one another regarding our growing-up years.

As a new mom, I was haunted by a feeling that something terrible could happen to one of my daughters. To comfort myself, I took them every single Friday to visit their pediatrician. Dr. Jane was wise, grandmotherly, and she would look at each of my girls, rub their backs and listen with her stethoscope as I held each daughter to my chest.

Dr. Jane would put her stethoscope to my ears so I could listen. This would reassure me for the next few days, but by the very next Friday, I would arrive with my daughters at her office. We went through this same routine each Friday for the first year of my daughters' lives. Dr. Jane would help carry my daughters out to our van, I would drive us down the island from Coupeville, stopping at South Whidbey State Park to take my girls for a stroller ride.

My fear was not something I could control. My babies felt vulnerable. Constipation, coughing, stuffed noses, the pain from teething, ear infections, rashes . . . how does any first-time mother know how to cure all these things? How does any first-time mother know their baby will recover? And it was more terrifying with twins because there were twice the number of coughs, fevers, rashes and ear infections.

Many first-time mothers have their own moms to call for reassurance. A lifelong drug addict with serious mental illness, my mother could not stand in those shoes for me. Grammy and Poppy had done their best to give my brother and I stability and love growing up, but they couldn't face the truth about our mother, which meant we were exposed to her repeatedly. Worse, when I reconnected with my father, my grandparents refused to tolerate me having a relationship with my father. This time, when forced to choose, I chose my father. And my grandparents refused to have any contact with me. Another loss.

When I decided to move forward with the Lions to buy a shelter, I had to be braver than I felt, and act more capable than I was — something I had been doing since I was very young. I faced fear with fierceness.

I covered up a feeling of unworthiness. I imagined the lions of the New York Public Library guarding me. I was a lion out front.

Fierce no matter what my family threw at me.

Fierce no matter what the state mandated of Cocoon.

Fierce no matter the bank account.

It could have been scary, and I could have been terrified shitless, but I didn't feel that. I didn't know how to feel that.

I was adding a big load on the tiny shoulders of the little girl inside of me by asking her to take on the youth shelter.

It would take a few more years before I could see my own fragility and learn to stop covering fear with fierceness.

9

IT RAINS

Whidbey Island

There are things about the Pacific Northwest that have changed me, changed every cell in my body. The rain, for one. Much of the year, the sky is cloud-covered. When the clouds finally parted one spring, and my daughter Aliza was walking and talking, she pointed up at the sky, her eyebrows furrowed. "Mommy, what's that?" She was pointing to the sun. In her short two years of life, she had seen so little of it.

I grew up with rain on Long Island in New York. We had summer rain, thunder and rain, rainstorms, pouring-down rain, drizzle, raining cats and dogs, rain mixed with snow and rain coming down in sheets. None of that was like the Pacific Northwest rain on Whidbey Island.

Whidbey Island rain was sometimes over here and later over there. It could be raining on one street, but you'd turn the corner, and it wouldn't be raining one block over.

"Gonna rain" was part of the standard greeting on the island. I misunderstood and thought the locals were always warning me that it would rain soon. I took the sentence literally, like I needed to prepare for something. Then I realized it wasn't a suggestion. It was more like the way islanders said hello and made a joke. It was always "gonna rain."

Most of the time, all year round, we have mist. I can almost always feel a wetness on my skin when I am outside. The mist is so subtle, Pacific Northwesterners will swear it's not raining. But I feel it, my hair absorbs it, and I am sprinkled with it like just a touch of perfume: mist, a faint scent of salt, cedar, sea and smoke.

Occasionally, there is Holy Shit Rain. This is a rain attack; you must pull your car over and you can't drive in it. Your wipers can't keep the windshield clear. If you don't stop, you may run off the road, or your car will float on the pools of water on the road, and you'll spin out.

Our house on the island had a metal roof. The metal roof amplified the sound of the rain. Anywhere I was in the house, I could hear the rain drumming to different beats on the roof. Melodic at first, then tiring. I turned on the stereo to cover the sound of the rain.

To me, the rain was all-embracing and relentless. She was a constant. Present, reliable, steady. Sometimes reassuring. Pacific Northwesterners always talk about the rain. "Still raining," they say – Pacific Northwest humor.

At least once a year, we get the River of Rain. This is exactly what it sounds like. Instead of the "here-and-there" rain, the River of Rain goes everywhere, covering everything and bringing the floods.

Rarely, but it happens, we get a Did You Hear That Thunder? On the East Coast, I grew up with thunder and lightning – they were part of the humid summers of my childhood. In the Pacific Northwest, thunder and lightning are rare. When it happens, everyone stops to listen. It is an event.

They stop the same way when it snows. Just a few flurries in the Pacific Northwest, and everyone is still. East Coast visitors laugh at us. But there is wisdom in the Northwestern mind. The constant wetness in our air keeps our roads wet. When the temperature drops, our roads ice over. The Northwesterners know to stay off the roads when it snows, because just below the snow, our roads are deadly.

I learned to leave my East Coast mindset behind. It didn't serve me in the west. I'd tried to do the same with my childhood – leave it on the East Coast. The things I experienced didn't seem to apply to my adult life. As a marriage and family therapist, I wanted to create a new, healthier branch of the family, leaving behind addictions, delusions, narcissism, violence, child abuse and paranoia.

In the pink house of my childhood, when it rained, my grandfather's paranoid delusions often surfaced. He was a retired firefighter. He had faced many blazes, run into burning buildings, saved people and witnessed tragedies. It took courage to go into a burning building.

Yet the man I knew did not seem brave; he was filled with terror whenever it rained, and delusional when the rain was accompanied by thunder and lightning. He unplugged every single electrical thing in the house. Shut down the breaker. Sat up all night in his rocking chair, a drink in his hand and a baseball bat in his lap. He was certain the house would catch on fire. The baseball bat was for looters.

My grandmother would try to calm him, speaking only in Yiddish. The phrase I understood as a child was *"ir zent dershrokn di kinder"* – you are scaring the children. As she tried to calm him, he often took a swing at her, becoming louder and more violent. *"Meshuggeneh!"* – you are crazy. She retreated to her bedroom, telling me and my brother to do the same from behind her closed door.

I understood my grandfather had storms in his head. Like rain, his storms came and went.

When I moved into our home on Whidbey Island, my grandfather sent me a box. Inside was a statue of a polar bear. It was his way of acknowledging that maybe I had made it to the North Pole. My twins had been born in a snowstorm, and my house filled with toys, like Santa's workshop.

When I opened the box and saw the polar bear, I lifted it onto my lap. The polar bear of stone. That was how my grandfather saw me: stubborn as a stone, fierce as a bear. Wild and unyielding to his control or anyone else's.

I kept the polar bear in the living room for a few days and then realized I couldn't look at it.

It was reminding me of all I had lost as a child, and how I'd searched for home, for my lost family. I put the bear in the hall closet, where I kept books and photo albums, and set it on the shelf as a bookend.

I got used to seeing the bear in the closet. The message from my grandfather wore off its paws and strong back, like a charm that lost its curse. The bear transformed. I saw the polar bear as the inner strength I'd needed to get through my childhood. I felt the bear inside me, preparing me for all I was taking on with the teen shelter. I would open the closet door and stare at the bear.

The polar bear was able to walk on the snow, no matter what lay below the surface.

10

SHOPPING FOR A SHELTER

With the promise from the Lions Club, I went shopping for a
house. I wasn't sure what a shelter should look like. I hadn't visited
shelters, but in my mind, I imagined a shelter was a gymnasium
with cots lined up. The word "shelter" brought up scary images of
windowless rooms, where food was ladled onto Styrofoam plates
from paint buckets. I thought of Charles Dickens and children who
were starving. This was not the vision I had for Cocoon House.

I wanted to talk with people who were more experienced in
running shelters. I set up a meeting with Wilma and Charlie. They
had opened both a women's and a men's shelter in Everett, so
I thought they might have some clues about what I needed to consider
when looking for a shelter for teens.

Wilma and Charlie were no longer running shelters. They invited
me to their home for tea. I parked in front of a white, simple house.
The house felt like everything I heard about Wilma and Charlie.
They were "salt of the earth." Their home was uncluttered, quiet and
plain. There was a lot of room for God in their home. Wilma and
Charlie had crosses and Bible verses displayed on their curio cabinet.
I brought my twin babies, and we took turns holding my daughters in
our laps while we sipped tea. Wilma and Charlie were weathered and
gray-haired, with white, wrinkled skin. They were deeply connected,
speaking a language of their own, like a pair of seagulls, mated
for life.

Wilma said, "We are tickled pink you are opening a shelter
for teens."

"We are tickled pink," Charlie echoed.

Wilma added, "And that you want to make it homelike – I just love the idea of a house." She gave my daughters each a salt and pepper shaker from the table to hold in their hands. I hoped it didn't go in their mouths. Thankfully, my daughters didn't try that.

I learned from Wilma, and Charlie agreed, that my biggest problem wouldn't be finding a house to turn into a shelter. It would be all the questions to which I didn't yet have the answers. With all their faith, they said, "Those answers will come."

From where all the answers would come, I had no idea. But while I sat in their house, I believed them.

"All of this has the hands of the Divine all over it." She laughed and looked at Charlie, who agreed, "Yes, the hands of the Divine are with you."

Wilma added, "You need to have some faith." She leaned forward and patted my knee.

I was hoping they could offer me something other than faith. I needed to know what they knew about running a shelter. I tried to steer them back to specifics. "What would you be thinking about if you were opening a youth shelter right now?"

Wilma looked at Charlie. She reached her hand out to me. I held her hand, while making sure she had a secure hold on my daughter on her lap. "Your biggest problem right now will be getting the neighbors to accept the shelter on their street." Charlie rolled his eyes to the ceiling and chimed in, "Dear Lord, help her with the neighbors."

Wilma continued with a smile, "No one wants to live next door to a shelter, and especially not a teen shelter." She shook her head. "But don't worry. I'm going to help you with that." She appointed herself to serve as fairy godmother.

Wilma worked for the City of Everett as the Human Services Director. "The Lord placed me in just the right place at the right time to help you. Isn't that right, Charlie?" Charlie nodded.

"That's right, Wilma."

Wilma said she would take me to the Everett city planners and figure out which part of the city's zoning would allow a youth shelter.

"I'm going to help you get preapproval. This way the city can't fight you; they'll be helping you pick where to put this teen shelter."

Fight me? What was she talking about? Why would anyone fight me? I wasn't a fighter. I felt vulnerable. I couldn't fight a city. I had two babies to protect. My arms were full.

Also, the city needed this shelter. The teens who were homeless had no way to fight back either. They were hungry, wet and cold.

When my daughters and I left Wilma and Charlie's house, I wasn't sure any of their faith followed us out the door.

Did I have faith that all things would work out? I had not experienced faith. I believed I had to earn anything I had, including love. I didn't have any experience that divine support was standing with me, the way faith escorted Wilma and Charlie everywhere.

A few weeks later, true to her word, Wilma arranged a meeting with the city planners. The meeting was on a day and at a time when I did not have childcare. But I feared rescheduling, afraid they wouldn't bother to meet with me. I packed up my baby girls and their diapers, bottles, yellow blankets, pacifiers and stroller. We took the ferry and drove to the meeting. I searched for parking and then pushed my sleeping daughters up the street, squeezing the twin-sized stroller into the elevator. It was just luck that my daughters were sleeping. I hoped they wouldn't wake up bewildered in a strange room to strangers meeting with their mommy.

The three city planners narrowed down the city to a four-block area and told me they would allow a shelter on any of those four blocks. I was shocked. "What about the rest of the city?" I asked, trying not to raise my voice.

"There are homeowners on these other streets. They don't want to live next door to a shelter. If the homeowners fight you, we will side with them. There won't be a shelter." The planners nodded in agreement with each other.

I was furious. I was melting down. What if I couldn't find the "right" house in those four blocks? What if a better house was on some other block? The Lions would buy any house I picked, and now the city was intervening and cut off almost the entire city. Where did they get this authority to decide?

Wilma intervened, "Sarri, they are helping you. This is good news." She pulled me over with my stroller, letting me know the meeting was over.

"There are plenty of houses on these four blocks," she tried to reassure me. She got up to shake the hands of the three city planners, politely thanking each of them – something I couldn't bring myself to do.

That narrowed things down. The city planners said all I needed to do was find a house in that zone and get a license to operate from the State of Washington. Wilma was giddy with joy.

I left the meeting pushing my stroller with a bunch of fresh problems strapped to my ankles.

I buckled my daughters into their car seats. I talked to my baby girls as if they could understand the bind I was in. I explained that there was no such thing as a youth shelter license in the state of Washington. This was like asking me to go meet with the tooth fairy and get a license from her. I believed the city was saying "no youth shelter," without saying no to my face. I loaded us into the van, popped in a cassette and sang along with "The Wheels on the Bus."

I wasn't feeling any faith.

***

The guys from the Lions Club phoned me and were dismayed that months had passed, and I hadn't found a house. I assumed they were losing faith.

I met with Bob and Tom to explain the new impediments. I expected them to give up on this foolish idea of buying a shelter house. But they doubled down. Bob seemed entertained by the challenges I was facing, like it was a more intriguing chess game.

Bob said the Lions would assign a club member to go to all future meetings with me. He said I needed someone who was experienced with bureaucrats. He picked a guy named Jim. Jim, in his 60s, was experienced with nonprofits, always wore a suit and had a heart for the idea of a teen shelter. He became my guardian angel.

Jim had grown up in an orphanage. A child during the Depression, he'd ridden the infamous "orphan train" to Bensenville near Chicago.

When American families could not feed or house their kids at that time, they put their children on this train – to travel alone to a place they had never seen. Bensenville's massive buildings housed children. I had seen the place. It had been converted into a nursing-care facility run by a friend of mine.

There was an invisible thread connecting me to Jim. When I looked at him, I couldn't imagine his childhood, but I had seen the place that was once his home. It was like I had time traveled to the place where he was once a kid who'd lost his home.

Jim understood what a kid who was homeless truly lost – on the inside. He put his knowledgeable hand firmly on my shoulder and said, "We're going to do this." I believed him.

This was the key: seek help from people who'd experienced the challenges facing our teens. People who had been orphans, who'd lost their families, who'd been in foster care.

Jim pasted himself to my side. I was now a "we." Our first meeting was with the Department of Social and Health Services, to find out how to get a license that didn't exist. I had no idea who to meet with inside the vast bureaucracy. Jim knew.

We met with the regional coordinator, and we brought along the County Children's Commissioner. Jim taught me the art of building an army of pressure to get what you need. He taught me to talk to the press. He whispered in my ear that the way to move the community was to inspire them.

Jim, with his calm, his suit, his handshaking and nodding to the bureaucrats, got us the imaginary license. It was a "made-up" license. What we got was a foster-home license with a long list of waivers to operate as a shelter. One big condition of getting the not-a-foster home license was that it had to be a house the Department of Social and Health services felt was suitable.

What does a suitable shelter look like?

I didn't know.

And I was certain they didn't know either.

I didn't trust the bureaucrats. How many rules did they think were needed to give a kid food and a safe bed to sleep in? What rules applied to kids sleeping under a bridge in winter?

Jim and Wilma, 30 years older and wiser, with experience and faith on their side, tried to mediate between the bureaucrats and my eye-rolling and interrupting and questioning the bureaucratese. They offered the placating head-nodding I was incapable of.

We pushed forward.

My shopping team got bigger and bigger. Now we had a realtor, a Department of Social Services licensor, a City of Everett planner, Wilma, a Snohomish County Children's Commissioner, Jim from the Lions Club and me. It had been almost a year since the Lions offered to buy a house.

One day, guardian angel Jim called me and said he had been out walking, and found the house. I raced out of the school to meet him in the approved four-block zone. He was standing in front of it with his arms stretched out like he was in front of the Taj Mahal. "This is it!" he said, smiling with certainty.

I walked up the steps like I was entering a shrine. I didn't want to crush Jim's hope. Could this be it?

I walked through, hearing in my head the noisy teens laughing and counting the four bedrooms. Jim pulled out his measuring tape and we surveyed each bedroom to be sure bunk beds would fit inside the rooms. We measured the kitchen and living rooms – there were two. One could be a welcoming area for the kids as they checked in. Plenty of room for a dining table to fit everyone. It had hardwood floors – easy to clean. A holly tree in the backyard that you could see from every window of the house.

Yes. This was our house. Jim and I hugged and cried.

He brought his son, a mortgage broker, to make the deal. All the white-haired men from the Lions Club came to walk through the house. This was their house. They bought it with proceeds from their bingo parlor. Their name was going on the deed.

It was all mine to use as a teen shelter. For how long, we didn't know. We didn't have a written agreement or a lease. We had a handshake. It was mine to use as a teen shelter, that was all any of us knew.

As the Lions' tour of the house was ending, Bob announced loudly, so all the older Lions could hear, "You will need to pay rent each month because Lions are officially landlords."

Rent? I had no money to pay rent. As the group of Lions stood by the door and filed into the stairwell, I asked "How much money do you want for rent?"

Bob looked at his group of Lions and said, "We discussed this. We all agreed." He looked at his shoes, which signaled to me there would no negotiation.

"How is $10 a month?" He laughed, and all the Lions nodded their heads and laughed.

We shook on $10.

11

OPENING DAY, JUNE 1991

Cocoon House

For Jim and the Lions, the odyssey with me had ended. They got me to opening day. Now, I had to prove to them I could go on without them and operate a teen shelter. The Lions were running a bingo parlor, not a shelter.

Paul was running the school, and I was no longer working there. I would need to keep going without his daily encouragement. In the time it took to open the shelter, the students I'd known there were all long gone from "The Dumpster." I had no way of knowing what had become of them. And they were all too old now for Cocoon House. But I could help all the other Clarences, Ivys, Emanuels and Hollis. I was on my way.

But I had a long list of problems to solve, and no answers for any of them:

1. *Where do I find money for staff?*
2. *How do I succeed at getting grants?*
3. *How will the teens who need the shelter, find the shelter?*
4. *What will Cocoon House offer that will help a teen off the streets?*

Those were just the problems I knew about. I would quickly learn there were plenty of others I hadn't thought of yet.

But I wasn't anxious about these problems. They were solvable. One of the life lessons I got as a child in my crazy family was that there were two types of problems: solvable and unsolvable. My grandparents, for instance, had invested their money, time and prayers in unsolvable ones. The problems of getting Cocoon House up and running, in contrast, were all within the realm of possibility.

I created a budget and pursued grants. I had never written grant proposals, but the questions on the applications seemed straightforward. I just had to figure out how to answer the questions I didn't know the answer to.

My lack of knowledge showed at the funding tables. I got a call from the City of Everett; the planner said grant applications weren't supposed to be submitted in pencil. They expected them to be typed. I said that I was sorry for the misunderstanding. I could take it home, type it and bring it back the next day. The city planner explained the grants were due by 5pm today, not tomorrow.

His firmness was confusing.

"But you have my application, and it is on time. I would just be typing it."

The planner exhausted himself trying to explain the rules to me and typed it himself. I reminded him that the instructions on the application said nothing about typing it. I was discovering there were many things about nonprofits that were assumed. It seemed everyone else knew the code, and I had to decipher every single word.

I didn't have many places to submit grant proposals to. Some foundations couldn't help us start out because their rules stated that a nonprofit had to be operating for two years before you could apply for funding. How could a grassroots nonprofit stay open for two years without funding? I had the nerve to ask this. I called grant makers and asked them why they were creating such impossible rules.

I thought it was okay to ask questions.

While I could tell some people found me irritating, I was making relationships with others – with those willing to take a second look at the needs of Cocoon House.

Funders also had categories that they funded. Some only funded arts programming. Others only wanted to fund building new centers, not operating an existing one. Shelter was a category, but not youth shelters, only shelters for adults. Children and youth were a funding category, but it was for summer camps, mentoring and tutoring, not shelter.

I would need to plead with funders to expand their categories to allow us to apply for support. Calling and having conversations led to meetings. In the world of grants and funders, I decided there had to be exceptions to every rule. There had to be, or there would not be any funding for Cocoon House.

I wanted the doors of Cocoon House to open as soon as possible. Even though I didn't have enough money, I placed an ad for a housemother. Since I didn't have a salary to offer, I offered a room in the shelter – housing – in trade for "light house cleaning and managing the shelter overnight." I received dozens of letters of application by mail. It was heartbreaking to read the letters and see how many people needed the housing and the job. Interviewing people made my heart ache, as I could only hire one person. I had no experience hiring anyone, and it made my stomach hurt to turn away applicants. I worried about each person who wouldn't get the job.

No one who applied had experience working with teens. I was used to working in schools with professionals. I had to go with the person I thought the kids would like and find nonthreatening. My first hire was a gentle, older white woman named Evelyn, who laughed easily. She was missing a tooth, and her back curved from scoliosis. She had long, dark gray-brown hair that fell in front of her face, leaving just the tip of her nose poking through the gray streaks. She was pushing her hair away from her face every few seconds, like she was surprised that once again her hair was in her eyes. When she sat down to interview, she pulled up her legs and sat across from me cross-legged. Though she was an older woman, she felt young to me, adolescent. Some adults are forever just kids at heart. Evelyn was living on her daughter's couch.

She was a homemaker who had lost her home. She was experienced with teenagers, having raised a few, and had a soft voice. I tried to imagine how she would look to a teenager – "safe" was the word that came to me. I traded her a bedroom of her own in Cocoon House and a small stipend for being the housemother, cooking dinner and watching over the teens at night in the shelter.

I got our bunk beds and furniture donated from Volunteers of America, where Jim worked. I had Evelyn to watch over the kids at night, and I hired a young college grad with blond hair shaved close to his head, whose attire showed an attention to detail, as administrative assistant. Danny was in his 20s, a big fan of Nirvana and had a great sense of humor. Danny didn't say much, but when he spoke, it seemed important. His sentences were short, often one word. I liked that. He didn't exhaust my energy with pointless talking. Not taking himself or anything else too seriously, he helped ease the burden I felt on my shoulders. Danny reminded me to laugh and would do anything that needed doing. He often spoke in gestures using his arms and eyes. He tackled all issues with me; he was willing to keep the doors open during the day, even though he had no guarantee that I could afford to keep him on.

It was not possible for me to commit to any shift hours, day or night, at the shelter, given my daughters' age. My job was to find our operating money, figure out what the teens would need, recruit and train volunteers, and create partnerships. We had four volunteers commit to the weekends, giving Evelyn and Danny relief from keeping the shelter open.

One teacher from the school I had worked at in Everett came to volunteer on weekends. I was grateful to have someone I knew as an experienced, caring teacher at Cocoon House on the weekends. She forged connections with all the kids we were serving.

I carried a pager 24 hours a day, seven days a week. Cocoon House would always be on my left hip in a little black box.

I had no experience as a leader or executive director. I was learning the job while doing the job. I figured it was okay to be learning as I was went, since it was not a paying job.

On opening day, Cocoon House had $40 in the bank.

Was I scared to open Cocoon House with only $40 in the bank?

Not at all, because that was four full months of rent. Plus, I knew we had $10,000 coming from the City of Everett. That would pay Danny and Evelyn and buy food, for at least a little while.

I was just plain hopeful the money that we needed would come. Every experience at Cocoon was teaching me that there were helpful people everywhere – I just had to find them. I decided not to focus on the people who said "no" or who wouldn't help; instead, I'd look for those who would join me. It was a waste of my time to listen to the naysayers. If I listened to the naysayers, I would be filled with despair and maybe even give up on the shelter.

I put my energy into looking for the believers, people who saw possibility and were capable of community-building. I gained strength from the Lions and borrowed faith from Wilma and Charlie. I saw resources and possibility everywhere in the community.

I was brimming with optimism. Though the problems the teens were facing were heartbreaking, I was guided by relentless optimism that the community could make things better.

As I spent more time around other nonprofit leaders, I recognized the optimism trait in others. While facing domestic violence, child abuse, homelessness and hunger, you'd think the problems of the world would make nonprofit leaders the most pessimistic people in the world, but the exact opposite is true. We have this quirky ability to turn on the high-beams of hope in the darkest of places.

I was often accused of wearing rose-colored glasses, being Pollyanna and naïve. While the world churns out war, hunger, homelessness and despair, I carried just enough hope that we could make something better.

I knew I was walking into ugly problems that I didn't create. But I couldn't tell myself these weren't my problems. I believe we are all connected. Community is home. Grassroots organizing is not something I had prior experience with. It took relentless drive. I did not have extra energy, but I was stubborn and refused to give up. I was like a dog on the Iditarod sled. I just kept going.

This optimism, beaming hope into dark places, isn't something that can be taught. It is a way of seeing and a way of being that you either develop or you don't. My sense of hope is the trait that suited me for the job of running Cocoon House.

***

The night before opening day, I had a dream. The Hebrew word *hatikvah* appeared in my dream. It means hope.

On opening day, I was helping Danny and Evelyn make the beds. We were talking about the idea that a youth shelter was more of a home than a shelter. I wiped down the tabletop and kitchen counter. I wanted the place to shine; I wanted to show off how clean it was. I was dispelling the myth that a shelter was a dirty, dark place that smelled of urine and ammonia.

I didn't know who I was preparing for. To me, opening day meant we were ready to accept kids for shelter. I had never attended an "opening day" of anything other than the first day of school.

The Everett Herald ran a front-page photo of the shelter and me on the front steps of Cocoon House. The article announced that the community was invited to attend our ribbon-cutting ceremony. Jim came into the shelter with two extra copies of the newspaper.

"Have you seen this?" He held up the newspaper to show me the picture of Cocoon House on the front page.

"I don't think too many teens will find us in the newspaper," I said to a beaming Jim.

"Are you ready?" He asked.

"I guess. Want to take a walk-through? I think the kids are going to love this place." I tossed the newspapers on a table and showed Jim how the bedrooms were all set. He poked his head in the bathroom.

"Everything looks great!" He squeezed my shoulders. "See you in a few hours for the opening!" He bounced out the door.

I hadn't planned anything special. I wondered if I was missing something.

"I don't know why Jim is returning for 'the opening,'" I said to Danny. "He's seen the house. Maybe he's bringing back some people to make it feel like an official opening. Can you go to the grocery store and find a cake? Nothing special, whatever they have." I thought, "Just something to offer Jim when he returns."

Danny slipped out the door and returned with a sheet cake that said "Happy Birthday" on it.

"Happy Birthday?" I looked at Danny.

He shrugged and smiled. "It's all they had."

We smudged it with a knife and decided that once we cut it into pieces, no one would know what the cake said. I figured only a few

Lions would stop by anyway, so the cake seemed embarrassingly oversized for the expected number of people. My husband dropped my daughters off at Cocoon House, and he was off to work.

Who goes to opening events?

I knew the press about the opening was good for us. It could help us at grant and funding tables. Beyond that, I didn't know why the newspaper put us on the front page. We hadn't done anything yet. True, for me, it had been a solid year of work to get the house. But opening day to me just meant we could start serving kids.

In the afternoon, at our official opening hour as announced in the *Herald*, Jim returned.

"Hey," he said. "There are some cars parked out front. Go outside and wave people in." I guessed that's what people in Everett do. I opened up the door and stepped out, thinking he was kidding. But there were cars lining both sides of the usually empty street. I waved. People got out of their cars and walked up the steps. I stood by the door shaking hands with strangers. These weren't the Lions. Who were all these people?

United Way was one place that couldn't fund us until we were open for two years, but the entire 13-person staff came up the front steps carrying bags of food. Patrick from United Way congratulated me.

"Don't worry," he said. "We have your back. Whatever we can't give you, we'll find for you." The County Executive Bob Drewel came and asked where the ribbon was for cutting.

Ribbon? What ribbon? Did people really have actual ribbons? I was clueless.

There was Seth, the prosecutor who was the other speaker at the Lions club the night I made my pitch. A woman named Mary Lou from the Children's Commission came, and she told me she was ready to join my board. "How many people are on the board?" she asked. I was too embarrassed to tell her there wasn't much of a board yet.

In fact, the whole Children's Commission came. Local police officers came, letting me know how grateful they were to have this resource. Mary from Child Protective Services came with others from her department. She offered to volunteer. All the teachers from the school I had worked at came. They brought useful things, like bathroom cleaner, toothpaste, shampoo, toilet paper, tissues. All the Lions came. Danny was going up and down the stairs giving tours.

The community cared about us. Cocoon House was a newborn shelter, and they showered us with gifts, checks, groceries and support. Each person walking in the door handed me something. Cocoon House had a family, and I was meeting them.

I wondered if I should give tours, but too many people were pouring in the door, so I stayed there to greet them.

One guy, in a suit and tie and very shiny shoes, handed me his card and said, "If you ever run into trouble, call that phone number in red. I will help you." His card said he was from the Medina Foundation. He was the first person I met whose name started with "General." I put that card in my pocket, knowing that you never know when you may need to call a general for help.

Paul came, the mayor of Everett came, the city council members, the school superintendent, other housing directors, the Red Cross, a group from the League of Women Voters and some Rotarians. A woman named Karla brought her newly hired team of teen advocates. She said they were working to help teens in crisis all over the county, and several needed shelter right away. She had ideas about how we could work together. A group of quilters came and had handmade quilts for each of the new beds.

My daughters, two and a half years old, were sitting on the floor by my legs, playing with their toys while people introduced themselves. Cocoon House was just another home to the girls. Paul scooped them up in his arms and carried them outside to play under the holly tree, away from the rush of people coming in the door. Evelyn served little squares of cake, cutting them smaller and smaller, until there were none left.

There was no space to turn around. The house – the bedrooms, the bathrooms, the kitchen, the living room – and the yard overflowed with people. Many of them knew each other.

For a moment, I watched the scene. Nothing had prepared me for this.

I had opened the shelter in such a caring and generous community. Cocoon House was on a neighborhood street where the houses were modest. The surrounding homes in the city did not give an impression of wealth. I learned that in this community, and in nonprofits, generosity and wealth were not tied together. Generosity came from anywhere and everywhere. On opening day, it poured down like rain on Cocoon House. Cocoon House was already part of something larger than itself. It belonged. It wasn't an unwanted blight. It was cherished — not only accepted, but celebrated. And for a moment, standing inside of its walls, I felt what it meant to belong. Cocoon House belonged to Everett.

The strangers attending our opening day gave me faith — faith that the doors of Cocoon House would remain open. I didn't think I would ever have the faith that Wilma had, but this feeling of welcome and belonging filled me with faith. It was in the air, in the floorboards, in the holly tree outside. It was breathing all around me.

12

METAL SIGNS

Cocoon House was freshly painted gray-blue. It fit in with the other houses on the street, but of course it wasn't like the other houses. There were houses on each side, one with a couple and the other with an elderly person. There were two houses across the street, each with single elderly people. The other houses seemed empty, quiet and lonely by comparison. Cocoon House was bustling with visitors and teenagers, adding vibrancy and life energy to the street.

The house number, 2726, was on the house, and we had the words "Cocoon House" above the house number. But the words were the size of my hand. We were on a neighborhood street. We did not have a big sign advertising we were a shelter. There was no bus stop in front of the house.

The kids we were there to serve didn't have cars and had to find their way to us on foot.

Putting fliers up all over town seemed more fitting for a rock concert than a youth shelter. Who would follow a paper sign stapled to a telephone pole to a house with strangers? If we were going to help a teenager with survival skills, did we want to teach them to look for fliers written by strangers and go God-knows-where? No.

I walked around the streets of downtown Everett and looked at the businesses, sidewalks and parking lots from the perspective of a teen. How would they know there was a youth shelter to go to? As I walked the streets, I noticed the metal signs: street signs, bus signs. I called the city planner, one who gave me the four-block zone, and asked if the city could make metal signs so that our shelter would look more legitimate. He readily said, "Sure," the way you would say yes to help a friend. I noticed that his attitude toward me had shifted. Maybe I could be more patient with people as they warmed to Cocoon House.

The city had its own sign-making shop. They made metal signs in white with blue lettering: Cocoon House Teen Shelter and our phone number. The city planner called me when the signs were ready and asked where I thought they should put them. How far we had come together! I was being asked, not told. I was leaving the four-block radius.

I drove around the city and identified some streets, deciding on the bus stops. The metal signs looked more trustworthy than a flyer. We had a phone number kids could call. When a kid called, we would send a cab to pick up them up wherever they were.

After metal signs went up at bus stops all over one city, other nearby cities called me asking for the metal signs, and they went up in nearby cities and rural towns.

Karla and her team of teen advocates got familiar with the bridges, woods and boarded-up houses where teens were living. Karla and I strategized ways to make our two resources stretch the furthest in our sprawling county. Karla, with her luminous bright blue eyes, black hair curled and set in place, came weekly to meet at the kitchen table in the shelter. She wore tailored suits with skirts – overdressed, I thought, for serving kids – while I wore my usual black pants and plain shirt. This was as dressed up as I ever got for work. Karla looked like she took her job and professionalism seriously. I was a mommy of twins who sometimes discovered I had my shirt on backward or I was wearing two different shoes when I got to work. My hair could spring out, going in all directions, while she had every strand set in hot rollers, perfectly in place. Karla conveyed patience and respect, while I downed my coffee, trying to be more alert than I felt.

I had the shelter, and Karla had a team of four people working out of their cars. They were outreach, and we were the shower, food and safe harbor. The teen advocates would pack their trunks with food and clean clothes. Their job was to build trust with kids who were homeless. Karla was navigating a whole different set of problems than those I was dealing with. Karla's list of problems:

1. Hiring trustworthy people to drive around with kids in their cars
2. Getting insurance for vehicles owned by the staff
3. Figuring out how to win the trust of a teen
4. Offering a service that had no license
5. Learning how to deal with violent and abusive families whose kids were trying to get away
6. Dealing with other organizations that wanted the advocates for teens to do other things, not part of their actual jobs

Rather than keep a bravado of distance, proving to one another we were each capable, Karla and I were honest with each other. We laid her problems and mine on the table. We shared the problems we were facing and brainstormed solutions together. Trust was growing as we combined what we knew. If a problem got one of our programs in trouble, we stood up for each other. Karla and I were strategic, prepared, armed with stories, facts, statistics and details. We shared what we learned. While sharing program problems and solutions, we also shared trainings for our staff. Though we were from two different organizations, Karla and I were pouring the cement and laying the foundation together for both programs.

The teen advocates became a life ring floating in the waves, trying to save teens from drowning. When a teen trusted an advocate, they would eventually try a night at Cocoon House. Local high schools and the school where I previously worked always had kids who needed the shelter, too.

The kids who found their way to the steps of the "shelter" weren't really sure what a shelter was. They would often sit on the steps outside. Our front greeting room had a large window view of the steps and the street. Danny, Evelyn or I would notice if a kid was hanging out. The kids would not knock on the door. The shelter started on the cement steps, buffered by heavy leaves of ivy. Gradually, we'd talk our way off the steps and into the house.

The kids didn't want to rely on help from Cocoon House. This was defeat and surrender. It was like losing their last bit of self-reliance to come to us.

I got used to looking at filthy, torn clothes; sneakers with holes; scabs on their hands; dirt on their skin and under their nails. The kids who landed on the steps were Black, white, Latinx, Asian, Native American, and every combination of these. Many kids were mixed race. They were gay, straight and nonbinary. They were greeted at Cocoon by three white staff, in the beginning. As our staff team grew, we grew in diversity. The kids came from all different backgrounds, different places. Some cruised up and down the I-5 corridor. The kids were not necessarily "from here." But they were here now.

When I talked about Cocoon House in the community at clubs, lunches and events, people always asked me if I was scared of the kids. The question was bewildering. I never felt afraid of a kid. The kids were the ones who were vulnerable. Fear stuck to these kids like a second skin.

Their fear was another challenge: I had to devise ways to be with terrified kids without adding to their fear. I kept my hands in front of me, in full view of the kid at all times, and if I went to make a move, I got used to telling the kid what I was going to do before I did it. "I'm going to take out a piece of paper from the drawer and reach for a pen." "I'm going to walk to the kitchen to get you some juice."

Every second counted when the staff and I were working to earn a kid's trust. Danny, Evelyn and every volunteer and staff person learned to move this way in front of a teenager. It became as natural as breathing. We were aliens introducing ourselves, sharing a home with kids who were scared of us.

Sometimes a kid would stay, sometimes they would eat and leave. My heart sank if I heard a kid leave. I felt like we were failing. But I forgave us for failing. I knew we were learning, and there was so much we didn't know – yet. Cocoon House needed time to learn how to work with kids who were homeless. There was no manual back then.

And the kids were also learning. They learned that if they left, we didn't chase them. Instead, the staff packed them some food to take with them on their way out. Mostly, they would return.

An hour later, days later – it didn't matter. They returned. We welcomed them back and remembered their names. We greeted them like they were family.

Kids didn't always come by themselves to Cocoon House. Sometimes, a school counselor or a teacher would come to the door with a student. Once Cocoon House was up and running, I was no longer working at "The Dumpster" with Paul. Then, he retired and moved out of Washington. But I continued to work with ten different area schools, including several alternative schools, helping set up support groups for kids who were in emotional pain. As a result, teachers sometimes brought a student who had a black eye or bruised cheek, a kid with a backpack and schoolbooks. The teacher would ask for a tour and want to stay with the kid for an hour or more, checking out what happened in the shelter before leaving.

The teachers and counselors were protective, caring; they were nervous about leaving a kid with us. I understood. The counselors and teachers had no other alternatives. They could not legally take a kid home with them. I had been in their shoes. I knew the boundaries they were up against. They had already called Child Protective Services, just as I had with Holli. They couldn't bear sending the teen out into the street, but it was only out of desperation they brought a kid to Cocoon House. None of the caring teachers or counselors had ever seen a teen shelter, and their fear was palpable too.

Cops also came to the door at midnight or 2am. They would wake Evelyn and bring her a teen they found asleep against a building, soaking wet. Other times, they brought a teen they took out of a terrifying domestic violence situation. Rather than have the teen spend the night sitting in the precinct for safety, they brought them to Cocoon House.

I was not the only person who had had a teen sleeping under her desk. There were plenty of teachers, counselors and cops who had been the only person a kid could turn to. Before Cocoon House, there wasn't much anyone could offer. Cocoon House filled with kids steered to safety by people who cared. Once in the door, they were fed, soothed and listened to.

Caring, involved adults came to our door heartbroken, worried, needing to know we weren't a mirage. Could they call and ask about the kid in the morning? Could we help get the kid back to school the next day? Could we give them something clean to wear? Could we take care of their fever? They needed to know we were grown-ups: stable, sober, clean and stocked with food, aspirin, showers, soap, beds.

The community of Cocoon House grew to include school counselors, teachers and cops, as well as Karla's advocates. The pipeline to Cocoon house was built by individuals who didn't know one other, but were moving in tandem, like an army of ants.

13

RAVEN

I got used to looking out the window to see if there was a teen on the cement steps out front.

They landed like birds on a wire. One minute nothing, then I'd look out and see a kid.

One day it was the back of a girl. I opened the door and slid onto the porch. I held my coffee cup with both hands, keeping my hands in plain sight.

With my small size, my hair pulled back in a ponytail and my casual jeans and shirt, I was hoping to appear "not like a creep." I stood on the porch sipping coffee.

"Hi," I said. The girl was spread out on the steps, both feet stretched up, her back against the ivy, like she was stretched out on a couch. Except it wasn't a couch. It was a wet cement step. Her sneakers had holes from the top right through the bottom. She was wearing a T-shirt, wet and clinging to her skin. Her hair was as black as a crow. Her face was pale white, and her lips were blue. Not blue from lipstick – blue from cold. She was trying to look comfortable lying across the steps. Rain fell softly on her.

"Come up onto the porch, out of the rain. Would you like some hot cocoa?"

"How much is it?" she asked.

"It's free. Everything here is free. Come up onto the porch. I'll go make you some hot cocoa."

As I opened the door, she flew inside, right behind me.

"The kitchen is this way." I was used to calling out everything before I did it, speaking my movements so she wouldn't be frightened off.

In the kitchen, I filled the tea kettle and turned on the stove. I pulled out the round can of hot cocoa mix. "Marshmallows or no marshmallows?"

She nodded yes.

"I'm Sarri. What's your name?"

"Raven."

I knew not to ask any more than I was given. I assumed Raven was not her legal name. Having met kids who were named Locker, Skater and Grey, I didn't say, "What's your real name?" The first test of accepting a kid was accepting the name they gave us.

I didn't know where these kids pulled these names from, but every kid on the street had a street name. I didn't ask for last names. Street names didn't include second names. Last names indicated family, and these kids were floating without theirs.

As Raven sipped her hot cocoa with marshmallows, I explained to her that Cocoon House was a teen shelter. I made sure she understood we did not charge anyone to sleep there and repeated that we did not charge for food, clothes, showers or anything else.

"Why are you doing this?" she asked.

No kid had ever asked me that.

"'Cause I don't think kids belong on the streets. It's rough out there."

She sucked her lips in.

"It's a way off the street, but only if you want it," I added.

Raven then told me she had a pimp chasing her, and he couldn't know where she was. Could she stay here?

I couldn't tell how old Raven was, but with her round face and soft eyes, she looked around age 13 or 14 – 15, max. She told me she was 18.

I asked her when she was last in school.

"School? Let's see, that was a long time ago. March?" She asked herself. It was now October.

"What grade were you in?"

Forgetting that she'd told me she was 18, she told me she was in eighth grade.

Facts: 14, dropped out of eighth grade, leashed to a pimp. I looked at her hands as she lifted the mug of cocoa. She had sores on her hands. The mark of scabies. No needle marks on her arms. No cuts on her wrists.

Summary: In danger if she went back outside.

My mind circled. How could I entice her to stay?

I took her on a tour of the shelter. We stopped at the girls' bedroom. "Could I have the top bunk?"

"Yes, let's put something on the – " and before I could finish, Raven had whipped off her wet white T-shirt and thrown it up on the bed. I looked at her, shirtless in a purple bra.

"Let's get a dry shirt from the free clothes pile." I opened a closet, and there was a garbage bag of cleaned clothes on the floor. I dragged the heavy bag out of the closet. And Raven dove into the bag, scavenging. She was a large girl, and she found a big gray sweatshirt that said "Stanford" on it. She put it on. As she turned around, lifting her arms up to slide on the shirt, I saw a big black-and-blue welt on her back.

"Raven, does your back hurt? You have a bruise."

"Nah, that's nothing." She put the shirt on.

I wondered what her legs looked like.

"Do you have more cocoa?"

"Yes, and we have food too. Let's get something to eat."

I was trying to calm my breathing. That bruise. I wondered who that pimp was, where was he hiding out. I wanted to grab him by the throat.

Raven looked safer in her Stanford shirt. I thought about the family that must have donated the shirt, their kid sitting in a dorm room somewhere, probably not even Stanford. Maybe that kid went to MIT instead. And then there was Raven, who was black and blue and spending her first day in a shelter for teens.

I needed to know just how close to Cocoon House this pimp might be. I had to ask without spooking her.

"Raven, I know we will keep you safe from the pimp guy – I'm checking: guy, right?" No correction.

"Is he nearby?"

"Nah, he's way down by the motels in Everett."

I knew what street she was describing. Her pimp was four miles away, stalking a few blocks of broken, cheap, vacant-looking motels, where people walked around drinking from bottles wrapped in paper bags. The decrepit gang of motels was around the block from a hospital and next to a vibrant community-college campus. You stepped one block off the college campus, and there were degraded motels that rented by the hour.

Cocoon House was removed from the edge of town, where people were walking the streets, screaming at each other, pushing their belongings in shopping carts, where loose dogs ran along the sidewalks looking for scraps and defiant men leaned on racy cars, pretending to be rich. I thought of Holli, who also had moved from motel room to motel room with her mother. Maybe she and Raven knew each other. Holli would now be 19 and too old to stay in Cocoon House. Our license was for 13-to-17-year-olds. I still had nothing to offer Holli.

Raven was here, now. A hungry girl who some would call "streetwise." To me she wasn't streetwise. There was no such thing as a streetwise teenage girl. "Streetwise" was just another term that let us turn our backs on kids while imagining they had the survival skills for being homeless at 14. Raven, with her bruises, wasn't thriving. But I wondered how long she would last in Cocoon House.

At Cocoon House we were offering help without calling it help, disguising the very thing Raven needed because she didn't want to need anyone. She couldn't need anyone. It wasn't safe to need anyone.

When a kid has been abandoned, they pull all their needs inside. I knew that. Rely on no one: that was the creed.

And we didn't want to rob kids of their independence or survival skills; they needed those, too. So, we had to help without making it look like we were helping. "I was going to the store anyway." "I know you could do this yourself, but I've got nothing else to do right now."

Needing is the root of belonging. Is it possible to belong without needing? Cocoon House was a place to be and belong. Raven could only belong by letting herself need.

14

THE WATER HEATER

Some things can't be fixed. There were lots of issues that came with having a house that were way outside my knowledge. Anything that needed repairing was confusing. I had no experience using tools. Challenging? Give me a teenager over a socket wrench, any day.

The house the Lion's Club bought with Bingo money was at least 70 years old and had all the problems you'd find in houses that are 70 years old. I wouldn't have done any better in a newer house, but older houses have more things to take into consideration. One problem always leads to complexities, piping and wiring that can't withstand hammering one more nail into the wall.

Danny came in to work one morning and found there was no hot water. He called me.

I had no idea how to respond to that problem. Could he call back with a question about a teen, please?

But every problem came to me. That is what it meant to be the "executive director." The job was Administrator of Yeses and Nos and Mender of Misfortune.

All I had for the no-hot-water problem was, "Who could you call to fix it?" (Sure as hell wasn't me.) Danny came up with a handyperson.

The handyperson came over. Danny called me back with the result.

"He said he can't fix it. The problem is our water heater. It's too old. He doesn't have these parts."

Old-house issues.

"Darn. Can you find out how much a new water heater costs?" Another thing I knew nothing about: the cost of water heaters. But we had no budget for it, no matter what it cost.

Danny called back with a thousand-dollar solution.

"Okay, I'll come in and write a check. Let's get a new water heater."

This water heater blew my budget for the month.

Danny borrowed his dad's truck and hauled away the old water heater. Bye-bye, problem. I watched Danny haul out the dead water heater on a hand truck.

Danny installed the new water heater, but then it had to be inspected by PUD. I had no idea why. The PUD sent out a guy to be sure it was hooked up right. The guy asked Danny where the old water heater was.

Danny had taken it to a metal dump to be crushed. I asked if we could get any money for it, hoping to ease the budget blowout. But Danny told me to just be thankful we didn't have to pay to have it crushed.

The PUD guy explained the water heater didn't belong to us. It belonged to PUD. They would fine us for crushing their water heater.

A fine?

I heard those words and interrupted.

"Maybe . . . we didn't crush it. Give us a day to find our water heater."

The inspector said, "It should be easy to find, it has a tag with a serial number on it."

Danny tore out the door to see if the water heater that didn't belong to us was still intact. Since it had a tag, we couldn't just bring back any old water heater. No, we had to find our exact water heater. I got in the truck with Danny and we went to the dump.

Crushed metal was everywhere in stacks. There was a football-field-size area filled with piles of crushed metal. Our human waste is embarrassing. How could we explain all this trash? I didn't know where to begin to look for our water heater.

I asked a woman who was working. She had on a hardhat and was wearing bright orange suspenders. "Ma'am, have you seen a water heater come through?"

She bent over laughing. There were stacks of crushed metal, row after row, pile after pile. She smacked her hand on Danny's truck and said, "Your water heater is probably the size of a toaster now."

If there was a manual for executive directors, it would have a chapter for every darn thing you could imagine, but it would not have a chapter explaining that you need to see who owns the water heater before you crush it. We left without finding our water heater.

I reached out to administrators of the PUD and pleaded for mercy. "Please don't fine us. The water heater was a big enough problem." Like a driver who was caught speeding, I earned the fine.

But I didn't know not to crush the water heater. I would have gladly returned it to PUD. Wasn't this common sense? I did not go around intentionally crushing water heaters. Why was there a fine for such things?

Cocoon House couldn't afford my mistakes. There was no room in the budget for things I didn't know, things I couldn't predict and mistakes that would get us fined.

Another question people often asked was if I knew then what I would face, would I ever have opened Cocoon House?

Yes. A thousand times, yes. Though I was not prepared to do the job and learned by making mistakes, and I had to tolerate how little I knew over and over, I would do it all over again.

Cocoon House saved lives every single day.

It was my assignment to learn how to run it. A spiritual assignment.

I adopted a philosophy at Cocoon House that started with the crushed water heater. My philosophy was: Every solution brings three new problems.

Once I understood the mathematics of "each solution brings three new problems," I felt ready for whatever came my way. After the water heater, I adapted to the reality of being an executive director. I adapted to not knowing things. I could call and ask others. That was about it. There was no internet with millions of answers to everything. I was limited to what I knew and what people around me knew.

As I lowered my expectations of sweeping the place clean of problems and came to expect a constant hum of problems to solve, the job of running Cocoon House became easier. Every day, I had problems to solve. Some were easier, some I knew nothing about, some went away before I could get to them. I gave up on hoping for problem-free days. That wasn't my job. My job was to stand in the batting cage and swing, while one problem after another was pitched at me. Period.

I did my best with the water heater. I couldn't figure out why they even had a protocol for missing water heaters. Who was out stealing broken water heaters? Was that a thing?

After a meeting with an executive at PUD who owned the water heater, they let Cocoon House off the hook for the water-heater fine.

One of the biggest gifts came to me as a volunteer who knew how to fix anything in the house. I didn't know enough to look for a volunteer that could fix things. Tim was working as an engineer at the Boeing Company. He would soon lead their community engagement in Everett. He had dark black hair, bright blue eyes, and was fit, athletic. He wore white button-down shirts and suit pants. He looked like he stepped out of a catalogue, no stains or wrinkles anywhere. "Looks like you need some help around here," he said.

"What do you know about teens?"

"Nothing. But the house gutters are falling apart and that's going to give you some problems."

"What gutters?" He walked me outside and showed me.

"Do you know how to fix that?" I asked. I had no idea what it meant to have gutters with holes hanging off the house.

"Yes, I know how to fix all kinds of house things."

Tim took the house off my shoulders. He fixed, brought in volunteers, purchased supplies. He knew what kind of paint you use on the outside of the house. He repaired the soffits, whatever the hell they were. He fixed the walls where water was getting in; he found us a volunteer to rewire the house. Why did houses needed rewiring? I had no idea.

Tim came every month and did his walk-through, making a list of everything the shelter house needed. He looked in every room and walked around the outside of the house. He brought his own ladder and tools and supplies. He never gave me a bill.

I was learning another thing about the job of executive director. It was my job was to find people like Tim. Or at least recognizing when a Tim showed up at the door offering to help.

I learned from Tim to take time to talk with people and learn more about each community member I met.

Everyone had something to offer. It was my job to know this.

15

TEENAGE PROBLEMS

One of things we weren't prepared for at the shelter were the teens who came with babies in their arms.

The first babies we served were twins. The momma, Juliet, had blonde, short hair, and was 14 years old. We called around the corner to Volunteers of America and asked for a crib. We needed diapers, formula, etc. Even Danny, Mr. Calm himself, called me from the drugstore, clearly rattled, to ask, "What size diapers?"

Being the mom on staff, I could guess at diaper sizes. My twins were three years old, recently bribed out of diapers using M&M's and raisins. The momma of the twins in our shelter was half my age. I wondered how she could take care of two babies.

How did Juliet deal with all her teenage worries, plus the fears of being a new mom with no place to go with two babies? My daughter Somer took one peek through the French doors at Cocoon House, saw the two babies and pulled the dress off her stuffed bunny. I wasn't aware the dress came off the bunny. I kneeled down to my daughter. "Somie, what are you doing with Ms. Bunny's dress?" Somer dropped the dress on the pile of donation clothes on the floor.

"This is for the babies. They need little clothes."

Oh, my heart. How could a three-year-old grasp the needs of little babies? How was it that she understood giving?

I didn't know how I talked about Cocoon House around my daughters. I didn't know how to explain the concept of homelessness to a three-year-old. What my daughters saw was that their mommy had two houses. I was home with them on Whidbey Island, and sometimes I went to a different house, and it was a house full of teenagers. And now there were babies in Cocoon House.

I also didn't know how a 14-year-old could raise twins by herself.

I thought of all the resources I had: babysitters, childcare, a bedroom with beds for my daughters, a husband, a housekeeper, a home and an education – a way to support myself in the world. I had a well-stocked fridge, a checking account, an income. I read books on raising children – heck, I had a degree in education. I read books on raising twins. I had a friend's mom who raised twins, I call her my Mom2, to call anytime. I had a mother-in-law, a father-in-law, my dad and stepmom. I had friends I could count on. I had healthcare, a pediatrician, a car and money in the bank.

We couldn't prepare Juliet for the life she was in. Soon, the babies would be too big to both carry at once. She didn't have money for the diapers she needed today or tomorrow. She could breastfeed her babies, but what would she eat? She couldn't apply for housing; she wasn't old enough to sign a lease. She didn't have money for rent. She was out of school and could not enroll in high school on her own with the babies.

I thought about what it was like for me at 14. I was a freshman in high school. My biggest concern was what to wear to school, and how to win back my points on essays in Mr. Levin's English class. (He had this unnerving system where you never got 100% on anything you turned in. He would give you an 80% and make you argue aloud in class to prove your case to earn your extra points on an essay. He taught us all how to fight for ourselves and to stand up to authority. I didn't know at the time how much this skill would serve me at Cocoon House, trying to win at the competitive funding tables.)

At 14, I was eating pizza, smoking pot on the high school front lawn with my girlfriends and keeping all my crushes on boys a secret. At 14, I pretended I could walk in high-heeled clogs; I pretended I could handle a date with a 16-year-old boy – during which I worried that I was saying the wrong thing every other minute. I pretended

I could handle the pot I was smoking. All of it was too much for me – the pot, the boys and the heels.

At 14, I smoked enough pot to get myself sick. I vomited all over myself in the girl's bathroom at school. My friend Erica took me to her house, threw my stinking pants in the washing machine and tucked me in bed in her green, peaceful bedroom to let me sleep it off. Erica and her twin sister Vicki lived around the block from the high school. I don't remember how Erica got me to her house that day. I woke up a few hours later to her mom sitting by me on the bed and stroking my hair.

"You have a choice," Mrs. Murray said. "You could have a beautiful life, or you could end up like your mother."

At 14, I learned from Erica and Vicki's mom that I could have a beautiful life.

These became the most important words to me, more valuable than gold. Mrs. Murray told me I could have a beautiful life.

I stopped smoking pot. I set my sights higher. I wanted a beautiful life. And Mrs. Murray became Mom2 for me.

Now, I couldn't imagine being a mom of twins at 14. What could I say to Juliet about her life? Could she have a beautiful life?

I met weekly with Mr. Calm, the mom squad of Cocoon House volunteers, Karla and her teen advocates to talk about the kids and what they needed. When I got to Juliet, there was silence. People were looking at the floor or staring down at the table. I had to say something, so I started pointing out her abilities. She was bonded to her babies. She was nurturing, patient and gentle. She was attentive, careful, doing all the right things with babies. Juliet didn't have a drug problem. She didn't have mental health issues. She wasn't out of control or full of anger. She was unusually compliant for a teenager. She was just a teenage girl who got pregnant, and now she had more than her two young arms could hold alone.

All we could do was help her through the day. The teen advocates got her back into high school. The school had a program for teen moms with a daycare center onsite. It was a start.

I needed to move on to my next meeting, about Raven and her school issues.

Raven shared a room with Juliet and the twins.

Raven went to an alternative school (not the same one where I'd worked). She went to class in the mornings and was getting homework to do back at the shelter in the afternoons. The goal for Raven was to get up to speed with her peers to enter ninth grade.

The guy who ran the alternative school was Stu, a large man, always smiling, reminding me of Santa Claus. He was coming to Cocoon House to have a meeting about Raven. We were the only adults around her, and I guess Stu considered us something like parents. I knew Stu from my days working at "The Dumpster." He was a good fit for the alternative school. He had a legendary rapport with teens who weren't rule followers. He had a good high-school-completion rate. He was patient and held high standards and clear, firm boundaries.

I figured things weren't going well with Raven if he was paying me a visit.

As I thought about Stu, I was expecting to hear the worst. Raven had a limited attention span. I pictured her being disruptive in class. She had trouble following rules in the shelter; I could imagine refusal to do assignments.

In the shelter, every request staff made to Raven was met with a "no." It took time to negotiate with her; staff walked away from her arguments, just needing to stop.

I pictured her smoking cigarettes in the bathroom or worse, the lunchroom. I worried Stu might have reached the end of his rope with Raven's feral behavior. But I knew he wouldn't give up; he'd probably step down a level and bring books and assignments for her to do her schoolwork full-time in the shelter. A last chance.

When Stu arrived, it was his first visit to Cocoon House. He asked Raven for a tour.

He was smiling, I noted. Good sign. And she wasn't rolling her eyes or refusing to join us for the meeting. She actually was engaged and looked happy to see him.

Surprising, from a kid I thought surely was about to be dropped from the alternative school program.

When the tour was over, we sat together at the kitchen table. Stu lifted his tattered, brown briefcase and took a stack of papers from it.

"Here it comes," I thought. "All her unfinished assignments."

Stu sighed and said, "Raven, I don't know what to do with you."

She laughed.

My jaw sank. If Stu the incredible teacher didn't know what to do with her, what was next? I looked at Raven, tightening my lips, signaling, "This is not funny."

He laid his hand over the stack of papers. I turned my eyes back to his.

"Raven is the brightest girl I have ever worked with."

I blinked.

"I have here some samples of her writing, her math, her grasp of science concepts. She is way ahead of a typical eighth grader. She dives in every day and breezes through the assignments, writing long essays and reading. My God, I can't give her books fast enough."

I looked at her. She was beaming. I was speechless.

"Wow," came out of my mouth like a lost hiker stumbling out of the woods.

"I want to get her into high school," he said. "Into one of the more challenging programs. She is so bright. She's ready for tenth, not ninth grade."

"This is great news."

He had some forms for high school. He left them with Raven and me to look over and discuss which school she wanted to attend.

"What a bright future she has," he said as he went out the door.

After Stu left, Raven said that if she was going back to a regular school, she wanted me to help her get the black dye removed from her hair.

She was becoming a kid. Raven for the first time wanted to "fit in." She was transforming from the hard, street-looking kid to someone who wanted her hair done.

I called the person who did my hair on Whidbey Island. I explained Raven wanted to have her hair brought back to its natural color. I made an appointment and took Raven to the three appointments it took to restore her hair. The black was partially out, and we could now see her brown hair. It felt like she was removing more than hair dye. She was trying to get the streets off of her.

She continued to break more rules at the shelter. I looked the other way, just wanting to get her to high school. I brought her novels to read. We talked about them. I couldn't keep up with her reading. She was often in her top bunk, reading. Sometimes I heard her reading aloud to other kids.

She was accepted into tenth grade. I took her shopping at Target to get some new clothes for school, gave her a backpack and got brown bags for lunches.

I heard nothing from the school. I knew that was a good thing. As the weather got colder, I took her shopping to pick out a coat. A real coat, one with a hood and some length to keep her warm as she stood on the street to ride the public bus to school.

I didn't know where Raven would live long term. She'd been living at Cocoon House for months. Cocoon House was meant to be temporary, for a few days or weeks. Juliet and the babies had moved out after a few weeks, when a church group stepped up to give her safe housing and the support she needed. Since then, Raven had had unfamiliar kids moving in and out around her all the time. It meant every relationship she formed was temporary.

Living in a group home, Raven was not getting anyone's complete attention. But Raven wasn't a teen who could find a home in a church group. Her cursing, rule-breaking and history of prostituting made her difficult to match to a family home. I didn't know where else she could go. We called all her relatives, and they each gave us reasons they couldn't take her in.

Yes, she had her top bunk bed, clothes to wear, books and a school to attend. But she was living in a teen shelter. She shared a bathroom with eight people. The phone rang at all hours, and she had staff people coming and going. It meant she was often exposed to head lice, scabies, coughing and fevers from other kids.

Cocoon House was full most nights of the week. Some kids returned home. But others could not. Danny would track down phone numbers and help the teens connect to relatives anywhere in the country. The kids didn't reach out and ask for help on their own. So, Danny became the person who helped them make a connection and a plan for where they could live. Danny became a master of placing, reconnecting, repairing or creating new threads of belonging. He wasn't trained in this. He had instincts and followed them. Danny put his ear to the ground and listened for caring. He then followed through, helping kids connect and belong. Danny beamed when a kid was moving out. He was the one who made that happen.

It was good that Danny did that job and not me. My mommy instincts wanted promises and assurances that these arrangements would last. I wasn't happy when a bed opened up. I knew one heartache was walking out the door, and another would soon be walking in.

Goodbyes were short. There was no time to grieve and, unknowingly, this would have consequences. One teen was gone, and another one needed their bed.

Danny couldn't turn up something for every single kid, but his batting average was better than anyone else. If Danny couldn't find the next place for a kid, there wasn't a next place. This was the case for Raven. We had to accept this awful truth. Homelessness was not temporary for some kids.

16

SWIMMING

Sometimes I left Cocoon House to take a swim. It would take only a few minutes to drive to Forest Park, head up a secluded driveway bordered by trees. The indoor pool was a small oasis in the city, surrounded by evergreens and walking trails. I paid my $1.50 and slipped into the women's locker room. The windowless changing room with metal lockers and a cold cement floor encouraged me to move quickly into my bathing suit and head to the pool for laps without delay.

Lap-swimming had a rhythm. That rhythm was uninterrupted. When I entered the water, it was the solitude I felt first. Though there were other swimmers, I was in my own skin, in my own lap lane. Swimming is a quiet sport, just the *splish* and *swoosh* of water. Swimming is a full-body stretch, my arms reaching through the tips of fingers, forming a small curve in my hand that pulled me forward. I alternated between pointing and releasing my toes as I kicked from my upper thighs and hips.

I felt my arms reach up out of the water, stretching slowly, exaggerating each movement, twisting my head to synchronize my breathing with the rhythm of my body. I held my breath underwater until I couldn't hold it in, and then I exhaled in bubbles, turning my left cheek to the side, tilting my mouth out of the water to take in my next breath.

It's the deep, long breathing that makes swimming laps so restorative. I imagine this is the breathing that yogis and meditators seek. It's the slow exhale that signals the mind and body to relax.

All thinking stops underwater. Cocoon House and its millions of problems stayed outside in the parking lot. After a few minutes of stretching, reaching, slowing and breathing, I increased speed, kicking harder and holding my breath longer.

The water was my oasis. I have been a swimmer my whole life.

When I was a child, I loved to swim. In the water, I was good at something: a strong swimmer.

I learned to swim at Camp DeBaun, probably at age 3 or 4. Each summer we would earn round patches showing what level we could swim at. Each patch had a fish on it: bluefish, dolphin, porpoise, sailfish, stingray. My grandmother would sew the patches on my bathing suit.

I'd earned all the patches by age 11 and could join the older kids for junior lifeguard training. The training was tough, as Craig, a grown man in his 20s, would pretend to be drowning. We had to save him in the water, stop him from choking us, wrestle him to turn him on his back, lift his chin out of the water. I had to fit my tiny arm across his chest to anchor him to my side and swim the length of the pool dragging his dead weight without having him slip from my grip. It was a huge challenge. I didn't feel like a good swimmer or a strong swimmer wrestling Craig. Sometimes he'd yank me underwater, and I couldn't breathe. But I knew he'd stop and not drown me. I knew there was no real danger, and yet we were practicing to face danger.

What an important thing to learn as a child: how to face danger.

Underwater was a separate world from the one above water. As a young child earning my swim patches, sometimes I kept my head underwater and cried. I popped my head up and realized no one could tell I had been crying. It was a safe place for my tears. No one around me could grasp what I was going through in my family. There were many times I couldn't grasp it either.

Above the surface of the water, I didn't cry. I made it seem as if it was all okay, no matter what. I didn't cry at home. I didn't cry in my bed. I only cried in the pool. Below the surface, I could cry and release something hard to carry around all the time. When I got out of the pool, I got to leave my tears behind.

The pool held my feelings. I had a relationship with water.

The kids at Cocoon House didn't cry either. I noticed that. They were in such difficult circumstances, and they didn't cry. I wondered if they each had their own secret place for tears, like I had when swimming.

17

WEDNESDAYS

When kids moved out of Cocoon House, I wanted their new housing situation to stick. But I also understood some might want to leave the new living arrangement and return to Cocoon, where they felt connected. I knew some kids would miss Cocoon House: the rowdiness of a house full of kids, the laughter and belonging, the sleepover-party atmosphere. They would miss the staff who had given them so much attention.

Danny and I created an extension cord to reach the kids who had moved on. We made Wednesday nights an open drop-in night for any teen who had ever stayed with us. On Wednesdays, we served a big dinner and played games.

A few returned regularly; others we never saw again. Some would wait months and then return on a Wednesday. It's hard to imagine how everyone crowded into the house on Wednesdays, but we did. It was as if the walls expanded for us by some miracle so that everyone could fit: inside, on the porch and spilling out into the yard.

My twins came with me to the shelter on Wednesday afternoons.

When I shopped with Aliza and Somer at a store, they always asked if we could get things for the teens at Cocoon to bring on Wednesdays.

Wednesdays were also time we had community services visit the shelter. The community health center social worker and doctor visited. The state sent Mary to issue food stamps, thinking it might help a kid be able to return home if they could bring their own food stamps. For kids who were thrown out of their homes and families because they were gay, food stamps would not help them get back home. But the food stamps did give all the kids something – it gave them a measure of security in their pockets. It was something they could sell on the street or use to buy food when they were hungry.

Our staff, whether or not they were on shift, often came in for dinner, too, and wanted to play games with the kids. This was never required of the staff in their time off. But they often wanted to be there for Cocoon Family Night.

If the weather was warm, we piled the kids into cars and went to the beach. I had been a camp counselor in adolescence; one night each week, I got to be camp counselor instead of executive director. I brought my guitar and copies of songs for sing-alongs. Some nights we walked to a park and played Frisbee, kickball and softball. We gelled so well together as a group at one point that we called ourselves a team and played softball with other nonprofits. Organizing a loose band of teens wasn't easy, but now and then we had a regular core group of kids who always showed up.

In fall and winter, we played card games or went to movies.

Wednesdays were sacred. Though it was just a few hours, they were hours that honored a relationship among us all. Wednesday nights at Cocoon said, "We miss you and care about how you are."

I was a member of the YMCA, and I thought they had a great facility for our teens to use on Wednesday nights in the winter. I imagined our teens playing basketball or volleyball, scooter racing and swimming.

So, one rainy Wednesday night, I brought the Cocoon teens to try out the YMCA. The kids were swarming around me like bees, interested and curious, but nervous, limbs wobbly about entering a new space. It was hard for the Cocoon teens to feel accepted. They didn't feel welcome in a lot of places. As we entered the YMCA, a diverse group of many colors, the kids huddled around me.

I took out my membership card and wallet to buy guest passes. A new guy – white, with dark hair – was at the reception counter, folding white gym towels and checking people in. He refused us entry.

I lost my cool.

Carefully articulating each word, I said, "I'm a member; I can buy all the guest passes I want."

The teens got anxious and disappeared out the door.

"Not for them," he said. Then the white man turned his back to pack away towels.

"'Them'?" *Wow.* The shock registered on my face.

"Pass me your desk phone; I'm calling Jerry upstairs." I was certain he didn't realize I knew his boss. He passed the phone.

The teens were sharing a cigarette outside the door.

"Jerry, who the hell is this guy at the door? I just want to bring the teens from Cocoon in to play basketball. He won't let us in."

"Oh, Sarri, he's our new manager, Ted," Jerry said. "He just moved up from California. Give him a break."

Smoke was coming out of my ears.

"Give him a break? I want to use my membership and my guest passes. He just made all the kids feel unwanted."

"Put him on. I'll authorize your passes."

I tossed the phone receiver to California Ted, with his preppy polo shirt and tan pants.

"Hey, cool down," he said.

"Never call the kids I work with 'them' again."

I went outside to invite the kids in. They didn't want to go in. Danny and I cajoled them in.

Whoever this California Ted was, he made a lousy first impression on me.

But Everett was a small city, and I was part of the youth-service-providers network. We were a small group that met together. There would be no avoiding California Ted.

Just as I expected, the next time I saw him, I was at a community meeting for youth services. Though I figured he'd turn up, I couldn't believe a guy in youth services would treat Cocoon kids the way he did. In my experience, the youth-service people were a lot like me: people working for very marginalized kids, of all different backgrounds and races. We didn't turn kids away. What the hell was California Ted going to do at this meeting? He didn't have any of the characteristics of a youth-service person. No one in our room would ever refer to Cocoon kids as "them." No one in our group would ever turn a kid away.

No one.

He didn't belong in our meeting.

I tried to talk with others and not look at him, but our group was small, about 15 people. Hard to avoid him. He was in a preppy polo and khaki pants again. Maybe this was what he wore every day in Y-land. The meeting was broken into teams of two for an exercise, and of course I was paired with California Ted. I wanted to walk away.

But acting hostile to the newcomer wouldn't look good. We were always recruiting supporters, so I needed to not make a scene. I sat with my lips locked and arms folded across my chest. "Who is the outsider now?" I thought.

He surprised me.

"I'm sorry," he said, extending his hand.

It would do me no good to hold a grudge, though I wanted to. I was filled with righteousness, privilege and anger. But my righteousness would not do me nor Cocoon any good.

I always needed allies. I couldn't afford to give up on anyone. It could only help the teens if I could gain an ally in California Ted. He was sitting on a jewel. The YMCA had tons to offer Cocoon teens: a safe place to be, art, dance, swimming, clubs – far more than I had in the shelter.

And they hired teens too.

I accepted his apology. We carried on. At the end of the meeting, I invited him for a tour of Cocoon House. He needed to learn who "they" were.

A few weeks later, when California Ted came up the steps of Cocoon House, he was definitely out of his comfort zone. I don't know what he thought was behind the door, but he had fear in his eyes and tension radiating off his skin.

"Come inside – it's okay." We were on my turf now. His fear made him seem like every teen who came through our doors. It softened me.

"Let me show you around."

I watched Ted try to take in what he was seeing.

"Kids live here?"

"Yes, Ted. It's a shelter." He was going into a trauma response right in front of me. I led him outside through the French doors to the yard. He needed air.

"Ted, are you okay?"

"This is so sad." He was turning his head away, taking a deep breath. He was trying not to cry. I sat down under the holly tree.

"Ted, come sit down." He sat.

"I'm going to tell you the story of how Cocoon House got started." I watched his face relax.

He didn't need to understand homelessness and kids. He didn't need to feel the incredible pain of seeing the bunk beds and jeans stacked up in the donation pile. He didn't need to see the diapers piled on the shelves in the bathroom.

I told him a story, giving him a chance to feel settled, the way all kids do when you tell them a story.

What I didn't see coming was that California Ted became one of the biggest champions for Cocoon teens. After his tour of Cocoon House, he and I met for coffee once or twice each week. As we started talking to each other, we entered a bubble where we were in one long conversation that continued on and on. Ted always asked about Cocoon and how the kids were doing. He learned about homelessness and what the kids needed.

California Ted had much more time to attend community meetings at all hours of the day than I did. I was home most days till the afternoon with my twins. California Ted became a voice for Cocoon teens in the many youth-service meetings, even pushing some meetings into the afternoons so I could attend.

California Ted had my back. Within a few years, as our friendship grew, we collaborated on projects that would make a huge difference for children, babies, across all the shelters in the community. Together we built scaffolding that was missing. Our partnership was intense and close. He learned to use the resources of the Y to help the kids who needed them.

He taught me that most people didn't understand or look closely at the issues the children were facing. He believed I needed to spend more time educating people about the issues of homelessness. He taught me I could get more allies if I took time to teach people what I understood, instead of assuming that everyone already understood. Ted's background was communications. While I schooled him in homelessness, he schooled me in communications. He taught me to teach.

I watched Ted grow over the years. He always had a few people under his wing. He was brotherly. He was also honest about his human failings. He didn't hold up a standard of perfection, not for me and not for himself, not for anyone. But Ted worked on himself. We talked about the personal life lessons we were each chewing on, outside our work. There were deeper things that we were trying to repair.

Ted took me to my first Adult Children of Alcoholics meeting. Our relationship had a purpose. We could lean against each other. We saw the little kid in each other.

In time, we each knew the other's strengths. After we presented together at a National Conference on Homeless Children, Ted took me to national YMCA conferences to see how we could communicate what we were doing with the wider world of YMCAs. We also traveled several times to All-America Cities conferences. I was mesmerized, listening to stories of cities working together to solve problems. Ted and I were even asked to take a contingent and share our community story for an All-America Cities conference.

I took assignments from Ted. The same way he pushed me in the early years to educate more, he pushed me to teach more of what I knew about leadership in later years. We continued our long lunches, meeting in a restaurant he called "my office." He could talk me into anything. I was in Ted's band. We did nearly every project together from the day of his apology on.

Once Ted got an issue or an idea in his head, he would not give up, no matter what. One of his ideas was to build a new YMCA. The Everett YMCA building was 100 years old. He was right; they needed a new space. It took Ted more than a decade to make it happen, but he did. It was the last thing he'd completed when he got cancer.

I learned from Ted that we are all imperfect and broken in some ways. And that we can help each other through.

It all starts with showing up. Ted showed up for others. He showed up for me. I showed up for him.

How we show up matters.

Wednesday nights at Cocoon House were all about showing up.

18

RAVEN IS MISSING

One Wednesday, Raven didn't come back from school. This didn't seem unusual. I thought about all the times she wandered in late, broke house rules. She wasn't someone who reliably returned to Cocoon House at the same time every day.

But when dinner came and went, I felt concerned. No call from Raven. What made me suspicious was the other kids at the dinner table. No one was asking where Raven was.

I noted that and went home. I asked Evelyn, the housemother, to call me when Raven got in, so I'd know the time and plan to have a discussion and extra chores lined up as a consequence for rolling in so late.

At home, my girls were ready for snuggles and bedtime stories. We piled up all the stuffed animals to hear the stories too. I settled into the stories and did all the voices of the characters. I tucked them into bed. I looked at the moon outside their window. Hugs and kisses, their silken hair against my cheek.

No call from the shelter. I assumed things had just gotten very busy and Evelyn didn't have time to call. I read, showered and laid down on the bed with a book and Socrates.

I looked at the clock one last time before bed. No call.

In the morning, I was up early. I waited until 8am to call Cocoon House and find out what time Raven got in. Danny, who by this time was on duty, told me she hadn't come home.

I called her school to check on attendance. She was not in school. "Was she there yesterday?"

"No."

I wasn't worried that something had happened to her. I guessed Raven was skipping school and didn't want to return to Cocoon House yet, that she didn't want to face the consequences of playing hooky.

I went on with my morning with my daughters.

When I got to the shelter in the afternoon, I called in each of the girls, one at a time, who roomed with Raven. Talia or Monique would know something.

As I interviewed each girl, they denied knowing anything about where Raven was. But an hour later, Monique changed her story.

"Raven went off with some guy she knew. She was working." I sat listening, knowing not to ask questions when a teen was disclosing – just wait and see what gets spilled.

I looked at Monique, my mouth closed, just silence.

Wait in quiet with a teen, and they continue to talk.

"She's at Sugar's, or Undercover," Monique confessed, breaking the boundary between teen world and adult world. I never pretended to be part of the teen world, the way some adults try to hang on to it. I was only 18 years older, but I felt much older than the teens.

Raven, who was often on my mind and got more attention from me than any other teens, who had lived at Cocoon House for eight months, was at one of two strip clubs.

My only thought was to find her and drag her ass off the stripper stage. But having never been in a strip club, I wasn't sure how I would drag a naked teen girl who was taller and stronger than me out the door.

I needed a better plan. First, I had to figure out which strip club she was in. I didn't want to sit in the two strip clubs, hour after hour, waiting to see if she came out. One look at me and she'd take off.

I needed a better plan.

My body felt over-caffeinated as I drank another cup. Energy and rage were building up in every part of my body. Danny volunteered to go into Sugar's and check out the scene. I couldn't just do nothing. I would go to Undercover.

I waited to drive over to Undercover myself, alone, at 10pm. I missed the nighttime routine with my daughters and let their dad tuck them in. I needed to find Raven.

When I pulled into the Undercover parking lot, I was stunned at how big the place was. I must have passed it before. It was on a main road, yet I'd never noticed the building. It had no windows and was painted high-gloss black. "Undercover" was written in big white letters outlined in purple. I wondered what connection the name had to the strip club. But a strip club wasn't the place to look for deep meaning.

I parked my car and just watched the parking lot and the door. Maybe this was something I'd learned watching *Columbo*. The title character was a fictional detective I admired for his brilliance when I was a teenager. The only thing missing was a sandwich. Columbo always staked out his places with a sandwich.

After watching the black building for a while, I noticed something. The place had a side door. No one was going in and out of that door. Finally, a young girl dressed in fishnet stockings, a teddy fake-fur coat and shiny black vinyl short-shorts walked out of the side door.

Perhaps it was a stage door for employees?

That would be the door I would go to.

I got out of my car, walked to the black door trimmed in purple and knocked. Wow, that hurt my hand. It was a metal door. So, I kicked it with my boot. No answer. I started banging on it with an open hand. I wished I had a baseball bat. And then the door opened. A bald guy as big as a piano stepped sideways through the open door.

"What do you want?"

I realized I must look like someone's pissed-off wife. Piano man blocked the doorway completely.

"I'm looking for a girl. She works here. She's underage —"

"No can do. We don't have anyone underage in here," said Piano Man.

As fast as I could, I described her. "She's just a kid. She's 15 years old. She has long brown hair. She has big brown eyes and very pale white skin. She's in tenth grade!"

"No one underage works here. Now leave or I'll call the cops."

That just blew the top of my head off.

"You're going to call the cops? Oh, please, please, call the fucking cops. I have the chief of police on speed dial. How about if I call him for you? In fact, you know what? That's the best idea I've heard all day!"

Piano man went back behind the metal door. It slammed shut. I yelled every curse word I could into the air. I looked like a psychotic person. Piano Man had a good idea.

I went back to my car and headed back home. I called the police and expected they would raid the place and pull Raven out by her hair.

When I spoke to the police, let's just say they were not eagerly planning a raid. The police took it as seriously as if I told them my goldfish died.

I would take this up with the police chief when he came back on duty the next day.

When I called Chief, he invited me to meet him at his office. "Sometimes you have to talk to the boss," I thought. Having missed the night with my girls, I didn't want to miss any of the next afternoon, so I brought them with me on the ferry to meet with Chief. We would hit the Forest Park farm for kids after. I brought little puzzles for my girls to play with while Chief and I talked. He sat behind a huge, brown, wooden desk. His was a big office with lots of empty floor space. I unpacked a backpack of puzzles and snacks and set my daughters loose on the floor. I sat in the chair across from Chief.

"Start at the beginning," he said.

So, I told him about the original pimp – some guy with a gold tooth and a purple suit. I told him about her getting into school and being smart. I ended with the strip club Undercover.

Chief wrote some notes as I talked. He put the pen down.

"What do you think should happen?"

I described the raid, just as I would picture Columbo doing it.

Chief sighed and rolled his eyes. With his wavy blond hair – a bit long for a police chief – I thought he looked like an old surfer dude. Salty, weathered and kind, he patiently listened.

Then, he told me why he would not raid Undercover. He explained to me that there are very big things he needs to "extract" from these kinds of places from time to time. Raven could be long gone up the road by now. He had no evidence she was working there.

I pleaded with him, emphasizing her age.

He asked if I had ever been in a strip club. I said no.

He said, "It shows."

He then told me he was grateful I was doing the work I was doing. "We need people like you to care about these kids and you do. You are going to win some and lose some. Get used to it. It comes with the job."

My heart sank with the weight of this truth. He was right. In a column in my head, I moved Raven from the success column to the failure column. I'd failed with her.

I brought my daughters to the petting farm at a nearby park. Their joy was contagious. I slipped into the precious realm with them, touching and feeding the animals, their soft noses nuzzling our hands.

I went back to Cocoon House and met the newest kids who had just checked in. I felt a heavy weight inside. My daughters ate dinner with me at the table with the teens. All the kids liked having Somer and Aliza around. After dinner, I packed us up to leave.

On our way out, I found Raven on the steps.

"Hey, Raven." My heart fluttered. I tried to act cool, not concerned.

"I came to say goodbye." She threw her arms around me while I had my daughters in each hand. She pulled me over with the force of her hug. I looked into her eyes.

"Raven, please don't go. Don't quit. Your only way out to a better life is school. I promise you, school is the way out of this."

"I hear ya. But I gotta go now. I just came by 'cause I wanted to thank you. Thank you for everything."

She had a big smile on her face. I watched her turn and go. She was walking to what she thought was complete freedom.

"Raven," I called out, "if you ever change your mind, please come back." She waved to me.

I never saw her again.

19

LUKE

The purple door to Cocoon House felt like it was always open: new kids, volunteers in for a few hours at a time, staff coming and going for their shifts.

Eventually, the State of Washington created a real youth shelter license. I still needed waivers because the shelter license was written for larger facilities than Cocoon House. We had only eight beds, and we could run with two staff members on duty during the busy hours, and one overnight when the kids slept. But the new state youth shelter license meant we couldn't have a housemother. We had to have staff with eight-hour shifts.

Some people aren't a good fit for a tiny nonprofit with no real administrative structure. We didn't have a human resources department; you were hired at the kitchen table of the shelter. We didn't have a purchasing department; if we needed something, you had to run out and get it. No copy machine, no secretary, no car or van to transport kids. You had to have your own car and insurance to take a kid to an appointment. Every staff member had to wear many hats, common in a small nonprofit. But we were smaller than small; we were a miniature nonprofit.

I needed a steady staff willing to fix anything, cook, clean, delouse, pick up a kid, shop, make do with donations, stay late and be someone the kids could count on.

Despite the meager pay, it was easy to find people who were attracted to the work. But it wasn't easy to find staff members who understood teenagers and were comfortable around teens who had been in charge of their own lives for a long time. Many people were willing to do meaningful work where they felt like every hour counted. But how long would they stay if there was no way to move up inside the organization? We also didn't offer many full-time positions. People burned out working too many hours in the shelter, so part-time hours seemed best. Our staff needed time off to care for themselves.

None of our staff arrived with experience with homeless teens. Every hire, for any shift, needed training and support from me. Since I couldn't work every shift in the shelter, I would take our best staff and rotate them, with me as training buddy for new people.

The rotation of staff, kids and volunteers was dizzying. We worked on finding staff who would stay – the steadier the team, the more capable they were, and the more the kids would stick around and grow.

I gave up looking for people experienced with nonprofits. That didn't matter. I gave up looking for people experienced with teens who were homeless; they didn't exist. Instead, I looked for people who were patient. People who could sit quietly near a teen and listen. People who were calm and not inclined to worry. (Our teens would give worriers too much to worry about.) Staff who were comfortable around our diverse group of kids: kids of all colors, kids who were gay or straight, kids who were traumatized, kids experienced with drugs and sex, kids who were depressed and alone.

I found staff who managed caring without panic – a Buddhist, a farmer and a gutsy social worker. These staff members were the real walls, windows, doors and food of Cocoon House. It wasn't the house per se that the kids attached to; it was the staff. Each kid had their own favorites. I noticed that it didn't matter to the kids what color skin a staff member had, nor did their sexual orientation matter. Gay kids did not necessarily pick the gay staff person, and Black kids did not necessarily pick the Black staff person. Kids seemed to pick their "person" based on other criteria. Just the fact that I was a white woman running the program made it harder to recruit a diverse staff team. At the time I had some blindness to this problem.

Anyone who worked at Cocoon first came in as a volunteer. What concerned me most was not skin color or sexual orientation;

I watched to see if the kids were attracted to the person. Did they have the right blend of calm, warmth, patience and attentiveness? Did they like the kids, just as they were? Could they be accepting and inclusive? Did they do little extra kind things?

One day Luke and his caseworker came in; he applied to be a volunteer. Luke's caseworker was from the health department. Luke had sandy blond hair. He wore clean jeans and a T-shirt and red sneakers. He had me laughing in minutes. I couldn't understand why Luke was applying with his own caseworker in tow.

"Are you on probation for something?" I found it easier to just be straightforward with people.

"No, I'm sure this looks funny. I am offering to volunteer and bring someone from the health department to supervise me." I couldn't make any sense of this.

"Are you both wanting to volunteer?" I asked.

The woman with Luke spoke up. "Luke really wants to volunteer here. He's been depressed for a long time and has finally found something worth getting out of bed for. He wants to volunteer here."

Severely depressed. I looked at Luke.

"Have you attempted suicide?"

"No, that's not it. Well, maybe I thought about it, but that's not the problem. The problem is I have AIDS." He looked down at his hands in his lap. His head hung down. His eyes closed.

"I'm sorry, Luke. That is tough."

The woman jumped in, "So Luke wants to volunteer here. We realize you can't just have him volunteer, so I'll come with him, so you know he is safe around the kids."

I was very confused. "Why wouldn't he be safe around the kids?"

Luke answered, "Everyone is afraid of people with AIDS."

I dipped my head down to catch Luke's eye. "Not everyone. Many of the kids here are at risk of getting AIDS. You may prevent that."

Luke looked up. "That's why I want to volunteer here."

Luke and I talked about his "why." He guessed correctly that the kids at Cocoon were vulnerable to AIDS. He didn't expect to live many years. He called these his "last years." Luke was 36 – older than I was at the time. He knew he was going to die from AIDS, he just didn't know when. Life-saving drugs weren't available yet. He hoped he had two or three years.

He wanted to know he was making a difference, giving something before dying.

He asked if he could talk to the teens about AIDS, maybe have some educational nights at the shelter.

He could try it out, I said, explaining that I only kept people on at Cocoon House if the kids related to them. I could never know for sure who that would be. I told the woman from the health department that she did not need to come back with Luke. He could come volunteer on his own.

Luke and I didn't plan out how he would tell the teens or the staff that he had AIDS. We agreed he would decide when the time seemed right. One thing I was certain of, it was not my place; it was Luke's story to tell.

Luke was a thoughtful person. Thoughtful people did very well with the teens at Cocoon House. The kids liked having deep conversations about all kinds of things. Once the kids warmed up to someone, their burden of trying to not need anyone slipped away. Inside there was a kid filled with curiosity, wonderings, ideas, dreams and questions.

All our kids were explorers. They lost their homes early in life and were adept at wandering. They wanted to talk about everything. Including AIDS.

Luke became one of the most beloved volunteers. The kids adored him. The staff were relieved whenever he showed up. Luke's gift was making us laugh. Every time I looked at him, he was laughing or smiling. The kids flew around him like swallows. When we had enough money, I offered him a paying job at Cocoon House.

He was so excited to be hired, he threw himself a party at the shelter. He invited his support system to meet his Cocoon House family.

Luke offered far more than his experience of having AIDS. As he became part of the staff, he focused more and more on how to get a kid hooked back in – to school and to medical care. Luke made the shelter feel joyful. He played cards, listened to homework assignments.

Sometimes I would see him reading aloud on the couch to a kid. Luke made the shelter feel like a home. He brought supplies that he would gather from his AIDS support group.

After two years of working at Cocoon House, Luke became sicker. I cut his hours back. He came to work in a wheelchair, needing to enter through the back door to avoid the cement steps out front. Until he couldn't come anymore.

Luke was hospitalized.

One Wednesday night, all of us went as a big group – the kids in the shelter, the staff, myself and my twins – to the hospital where Luke spent his final few weeks. The teens brought drawings for him. The staff brought food and beautiful notes. I brought him a card deck to play with in his bed. My daughters brought cookies. We said goodbye.

At last, everyone left his room. My daughters were in the hall with Danny. I was the last to say goodbye. Luke took my hand and told me his final wish.

"I want my memorial service at Cocoon."

I wanted to pretend he wasn't dying. I didn't want to hear his last wish. But there it was. All I could do was receive it.

His wish was honored. We met the woman who was Luke's caregiver. I did not know that for the two years Luke worked at Cocoon, he had so little energy, he had live-in help. His caregiver told us how Cocoon House and having a job kept the sparkle in his eye. She told us how he would come home so tired, he couldn't lift his arms to get undressed.

Luke's support group came to the memorial we held in the shelter, as he wished. They brought cake and told us the stories Luke used to tell about all of us. They laughed, saying how small I was, for being the "big boss lady" Luke talked about.

The health department team that supported Luke from the beginning of his diagnosis, through his depression and to his last breath, came to Cocoon House. They wanted to thank me for hiring Luke. Hiring him was the easy part. Watching him lose his fight to AIDS was the hardest thing for our whole Cocoon family. After everyone said what they wanted to say and each kid shared what they would remember about Luke, the farmer shuffled a deck of cards and said, "Who am I dealing in?"

I stepped outside in the yard and sat under the holly tree on the chipped wooden chair with all its paint worn off. I listened to the kids yelling from the card game: "Nuh-uh – it's my turn." "Hey, don't touch that!"

I looked up at the leaves of the big tree and watched them twisting in the breeze, front to back. Two leaves twisted side by side like they were dancing.

I saw Luke beckoning me to get up out of my chair, as he always did when I was in the office. He pulled me away from the desk, turned on "Crocodile Rock" and sang along with Elton John while dancing with me. I felt his hand in mine, sending me for a twirl, shimmying, our arms swinging to the pony, hips doing the bump. Then, a slow dance while singing "Don't Let the Sun Go Down on Me."

I whispered the words from the song. Sitting alone under the holly tree, I allowed the grief to rain on me.

20

THE MOUSE

At three and a half, Somer and Aliza were fascinated by the book *George and Matilda Mouse and The Dolls' House* by Heather Buchanan, featuring a mouse family that lived in a dollhouse. George and Matilda were the mommy and daddy. They had lots of children and wore tiny clothes, floated in a watering can, painted with berry jam and had adventures in a rock garden filled with a community of other mouse families.

Somer, Aliza and I would talk about the Cocoon House, the mouse dollhouse and our own house. We were sorting out different houses by talking about these mice – at least, that's what I thought was happening.

Somer asked what mice ate and what they did at night. She was a young biologist, asking question after question. Aliza would curl on my lap and stare at the drawings of the tiny mice, talking about every detail, their little black eyes, the curled tails, the cart they rode in made from sewing thread spools, the tiny clothes of stripes, sweaters, overalls and aprons. No detail was too small for Aliza's artistic eye.

Around this same time, a strange, putrid smell was taking over our house, getting worse each day. I searched the laundry, the garbage, the fridge, under every dresser, inside every closet. I couldn't find the source. Until I did.

In Somer and Aliza's nursery, I lifted the lid of a golden jewelry box. The ballerina started moving when the lid opened, and she went around in a circle to the tune of "Edelweiss." Inside the velvet box lay a dead shrew, with bits of lettuce around it. There was no way the shrew got into the drawer inside the box with the lettuce on its own.

I asked my girls about the tiny shrew in the jewelry box. I learned it was named Mousey.

Somer explained she was trying to feed it. Aliza said it wouldn't eat. They did not realize it was dead, probably something the dog had left on the porch.

I rocked my daughters on my lap as I explained Mousey wasn't alive and couldn't stay in the jewelry box.

Oh, the howling that I was taking away their mousey. Their cries had me crying. My daughters had set up their own little shelter in their nursery inside a jewelry box and were caring for a dead shrew.

The shrew got a proper burial, flowers and goodbye songs. My daughters were inconsolable.

I couldn't protect them from their grief. I was powerless to make their pain stop. Their grief made me think about all the losses I'd had as a child, when there was no parent to share my pain.

Losing my family was continuous because they hadn't died. The loss went on and on. Confusing. I got on with being a kid without a guide for what to do with my grief.

I held my daughters as they cried. I couldn't take away their grief, but I could rock them and be with them in their loss. A tiny creature they cared for was gone. For a few days we talked about Mousey, we drew pictures of Mousey, we visited Mousey's grave, until the loss lifted. At some point, grief lets go of us.

I wondered how long the loss of Raven and Luke would stay with me. Grief can command our full attention. But how much grief can we shoulder at once? Cocoon House was a warm and joyful place. And it was also a place where there was loss and grief.

I could feel my grief in small bits of time. But I couldn't give it my full attention. I wasn't sure I could bear the full measure of it. And there was always more to do. While I was busy doing, my grief would flicker, like a faint star in the distance. Even if I didn't look up to see the stars, I knew they were there. My grief was the same, distant and at the same time present, like the stars.

21

LILLY ENTERS THE SHELTER

I walked in and saw the back of a girl sitting in a wooden chair by the door. Her brown hair was chopped short and uneven around her neck. It looked like something my daughters had done to each other's hair one day when they got their hands on some scissors.

A sleeping baby's head was slumped on her shoulder. Green snot was caked in the baby's tiny nostrils. I carried my bags, one on each shoulder, as I squeezed by the girl with the jagged hair.

"Hey, there," I whispered as I made my way into my own chair at my desk. "Is someone talking with you?"

She nodded.

Kim, my gutsy staff member, came from the kitchen carrying two warm muffins and a sliced apple on a plate.

"Hi, Sar. You hungry?" She was always offering me food.

I shook my head no.

"Sar, this is Lilly."

"Hi, Lilly. Welcome to Cocoon. When did you get in?"

"I don't know."

"Lilly and her son Will got here this morning," Kim said. "I was just going to get to know her a bit and see what was what."

Kim had mastered the art of not confronting or making any kid feel like we were going to come in as authoritarians in their life. "What was what" was Kim's gentle way of saying nothing and everything.

I loved the way Kim spoke to teens. I wanted to bottle it and give it to other adults.

I followed Kim's lead with Lilly – we were staying very general and not getting too close to anything hard for Lilly. Was Lilly even her real name? How the hell would we know? And the baby. When were we going to find out if that baby had a fever?

The baby was making a rattly sound, breathing through his mouth. Kim and I chatted, sharing a muffin, eating apple slices, making small talk. Lilly reached for the muffin, saying, "I'm starving."

There was my in.

"How about if I hold your baby while Kim gets you some food? Let's walk to the kitchen. I'll hold the baby and –"

The baby was tossed to me like a basketball. Lilly was up and bounding for the kitchen.

I reached around the bottom of the baby to get a secure hold after he was flung into the air.

His diaper was thick and heavy. Baby Will curled up his lip and cried, then gave up crying.

"How about grilled cheese?" asked Kim.

"Hey, Lilly, I'm just going walk to the bathroom and grab a new diaper for your cutie pie."

Lilly waved her hand. "Nah, that's okay, he can stay in that one."

"It's kind of heavy. I'll get him a new one."

"Whatever."

I scanned the rows of diapers and guessed size small. I laid the baby on the changing table, opened his soaking wet diaper. The skin on his butt was raw. A wet wipe might be very painful to him. I put a clean diaper gently on him. I turned him over and examined his tiny body for bruises.

I lifted his shirt, checked down his arms. Nothing. Only raw skin on his butt.

I felt his forehead. He had a fever.

I looked for a clean top and bottoms in the baby bin of donations, grabbed a fresh baby blanket.

Swaddling him tight in the blanket, I brought him back to the kitchen just as Kim was handing Lilly a grilled cheese sandwich.

"Hey, Lilly, your baby is so quiet. His nose is a little plugged. Can we see if he has a fever?"

Lilly looked at me while biting into her sandwich and shrugged. "He's not sick."

"I don't know . . . Can we check his temperature?"

"He's just always hot, and his nose is always filled with snot. He's a baby. That's how they are."

Kim washed her hands and wiped them on the kitchen towel. She wiped her hand across the baby's forehead. "Wow, that baby is hot. I'll be right back." Kim returned with the baby thermometer strip left from the health care doc. She put the thermometer tape on the baby's head.

"102."

Kim and I locked eyes.

Lilly looked up from her sandwich.

"Have you ever seen one of these? It's a cool new thermometer. It tells us if the baby has a temperature. The baby has 102." Kim's brow furrowed.

"SO?" Lilly said, ready to fight.

"So, the baby is sick." I said in a goofy Daffy Duck voice, trying to disarm Lilly.

"Can we check your temperature, Lilly?" Kim asked, sensing Lilly could be distracted with some attention for herself.

Kim grabbed another strip.

Lilly had a temperature of 100.

"Oh, Lilly, you are sick too."

"Lilly, can you and Will stay here with us while you both get well? I don't want you two going out in the rain and cold when you are sick." I asked, but was pleading inside that she did not go out the door with a sick baby.

Lilly shrugged.

"I guess we can stay for a day or two."

I passed Kim the bundled baby while Lilly continued to eat with both hands.

I walked back to the office area where the phone was.

I called the Community Health Center. I had the number memorized.

"I'm calling from Cocoon House. Is Carol there?" Cocoon House has become a code word inside the Health Center. And Carol was my contact person. I didn't have to explain anything to her. She had been to Cocoon hundreds of times. Carol knows if we call, something is serious.

"Hey, Carol, can you send someone today rather than tomorrow? I have a young mom and baby here who are sick."

Lilly came back to the office and looked me in the eye. "Who are you calling?" Threat filled her eyes.

"I'm calling my friend Carol. She sometimes comes by with a doctor when any of us here get sick."

"Oh, is she going to come see me?" Threat subsided.

"I think so."

I tried to act like it wasn't a big deal. I held the phone, knowing Carol could hear our exchange.

"Maybe today, maybe tomorrow. You don't know how long you are staying, right? Maybe you'll be here."

I moved the phone slowly back on the receiver. I didn't need to say goodbye to Carol.

I knew Carol had heard enough. She would have someone from the Health Center at our door in less than two hours.

I would be at the shelter for a few more hours. At least until I'd heard what the baby needed and run to the drugstore.

Fevers in babies were something I knew about. My daughters were older now; getting fevers just meant their bodies were fighting something. We stayed home and snuggled in bed resting and reading.

But having a baby and teen mom come into the shelter sick was a delicate situation. First off, we didn't know how long Will and Lilly had been sick. It also meant everyone else coming into the shelter would be exposed to the feverish baby and mom.

The doctor came and suspected Lilly had pneumonia. We had to convince her to stay at Cocoon House at least until she recovered. Kim made her soup, and we found her flannel pajamas in the donation pile.

Lilly told us her story in bits and pieces over the next few days. She'd spent her childhood in and out of many foster homes. Her mother had been hospitalized several times for long periods of time with mental health issues. Lilly wasn't in school much. She wasn't used to sit-down meals at a table. She didn't know how to keep her body clean. Her hair was matted, and she had lice and scabies. We had to require her to shower.

When she left her final foster home, she was 13 and pregnant. She hit the road for good.

When Lilly recovered from her fever, she took the baby outside in all kinds of weather – rain, snow – with the baby barely dressed, saying the baby always felt hot.

The baby's skin was hot because the baby was often running a fever. I caught Lilly trying to feed baby Will bits of frankfurter, though Will didn't have teeth and still needed mashed baby food. Lilly also filled Will's bottle with Coca-Cola. I thought Lilly was going to drink the Coke, but as she brought the bottle up to Will's mouth, I had to step in and swap the Coke for water.

We had to walk a very fine line with Lilly to keep her with us and not have our heads pop off in fury when she would stay out all night, towing the baby around town.

How was I different from Lilly? Wasn't I also towing my children everywhere with me? Why was I taking my daughters to meetings and having them sit through them? What about my daughters' needs? Cocoon House was needful, and my own daughters' needs always seemed to be met next to it. But was it a comparison? Was there competition? What would my daughters have to do to get my full attention from Cocoon House?

Among youth-service providers, it was a dirty and true secret that our own children were at risk, sharing their parents with other kids. Vulnerable, competing with the other kids who needed their parents. What did it take to get your parent's full attention – to become one of the needier kids that got your parent's attention?

Everyone was getting to know Somer and Aliza and wondered in their heads where this would lead. What kind of teens would they become, being around teens living on the edge? How would this affect them, to share their mom with others who "needed" her?

In Lilly, I saw the part of me that also had so much to learn. How to be both a mom and run an agency. I didn't have the answer. There wasn't an answer. Each day it was one step at a time.

It was hard to have a one-step-at-a-time plan with Lilly, because there were so many issues to address. But the very first step was to get Lilly to keep returning to the shelter. Getting Lilly to stay was a major milestone for a kid who had lost so many homes.

It would be one thing to teach a young teen how to care for a baby, but Lilly was defiant. She loved Will, but she didn't know how to care for a baby, and she didn't want to learn. Her defiance was scary. Will had no way to protect himself from Coca-Cola in his bottle or being dragged outside in the cold and rain. There is no room for adolescent defiance when a baby is involved. We wanted to give Lilly a chance to belong with us. We wanted her to have a connection and a place to be. But we couldn't watch her neglect or harm Will.

We wanted to give her a chance, but it was a lot to ask of the staff. They had to keep an eye on Will at all times while attending to all the other teens in the house.

All I could see was how much Lilly had to learn – but I didn't realize how much we would all learn from her. Hard to imagine that this scrappy, infuriating teen mom would one day teach us some of the most important lessons about love.

22

FOOD

Just before Christmas, December 21, an important meeting was held where the federal food money for the entire year was given to shelters and the community food bank. It was unusual to be invited to a meeting for money and not fill out an application.

For any other money, I would fill out six to ten pages explaining what our shelter did, who we served, how many kids we'd sheltered in the last year and a detailed budget of how we'd spend the money if we were awarded it. Every grant process was similar. After you submitted the grant, there'd be a grant hearing. At the grant hearing, every organization that applied for the money was invited to give a short presentation. A committee assigned a score to your presentation and written application. The money was awarded only to the grants that got the highest scores.

This process pulled out a competitive and perfectionistic side of me. I aimed to be the highest-scoring applicant at every grant table. If the Cocoon House application scored below the top five, there was no guarantee we would get the money we needed. If we were in the top three, we got full funding. I attended grant hearings full of anxiety, knowing that a bunch of kids and staff were counting on me. There was no room for screwing up. I had to be graceful, no matter what question I was asked. I had to be brief, but not rude. I had to have statistics memorized and be ready to explain policies. I remember one committee member asked if we served boys and girls in the same house. Yes, we did not have funding for two houses. And the need for housing is the same for boys and girls. We served as many boys as girls – a stat I knew.

I could be asked anything, but the trick was to educate and win the committee over to caring about Cocoon kids.

The only funding table for the shelters that was not a competition was the December federal food money. But I didn't know that.

After having competed with the local nonprofit adult and family shelters at every single other funding table, we gathered in our local United Way's community meeting room on the winter solstice. The room was filled with plush leather chairs, an extravagance I appreciated. Representatives from all the shelters – for adults, the domestic violence shelter, the women's and men's shelters, the family shelters – and the food bank were present. There was no committee to judge us. There was no ten-page application. There were representatives from the county, the cities and United Way – all watching, like referees at a football game.

I brought my daughters with me. The Director of United Way was thrilled to have young children in the building, probably weary from working with adults all day. He set up a table in the back of the community room for my daughters with crayons and paper, a game and books.

I sat at the big table. I counted 30 of us. I felt like a gladiator at what would be a bloodbath over federal food money. I was the only youth organization at the table. I was worried about how hard I would have to defend our very existence. I represented the only agency that was new to federal food funding.

For my sake, Bill from the food bank reviewed how the next two to three hours would go. He reminded us that if it took longer than three hours, then so be it. No one was leaving the room until we all agreed.

"Two or three hours?" I thought. I never would have brought my twins to such a long meeting. How would we survive such a long meeting? I called Danny to sit in my place if this meeting went on that long. I would just pick up and leave with my daughters.

"As a community we are given a certain amount for the year from the federal government," Bill explained. "This money has to last us the whole year. We have to feed all the people who are homeless in our community using this money. There is definitely not enough money to feed all the hungry and homeless, so we have to make it stretch."

He looked at me.

"We have to share it. This is a pie; it gets divided every year eight ways. We added Cocoon House this year, so that means our pie gets divided nine ways."

By trying to feed homeless teens, I was making everyone else's share of the food money shrink. I had added more mouths and no new food money. My competitive streak, fighting to get the most for Cocoon kids, vanished. I put my gladiator sword down. I felt sick. I was sitting across from the domestic violence shelter's representative. They had battered women and young children who had to hide in an undisclosed location. They were going to serve as many people as they did last year, only this year, they would have less food money.

My head was spinning, and I wanted to run from the room. Our grim stats were written on a big whiteboard. The total amount of food money was written on the whiteboard. Every agency that served people who were homeless was listed. Ed, who ran Housing Hope, suggested that the biggest bulk of the money go to the Volunteers of America food bank. While each of our agencies were serving numbers in the hundreds, the food bank was serving thousands. We voted to give half to the food bank and their staggering numbers.

Bill reminded us that any of our shelters could go to the food bank and get extra food if we needed, any time in the year.

That left 50 percent for the rest of us. I listened as other agency representatives explained the number of people they expected to shelter, how many they needed to feed. We each went up to the whiteboard and wrote the number of people we sheltered this year on the board. As the agencies described their numbers of people, I had tears rolling down my face. We were no longer standing in front of committees trying to win votes for our grants. We were talking to each other.

We were all in the same job. Cocoon House had served 175 kids in the year. The other agencies were housing 200–300. The men's and women's mission were much larger and serving more people. We had to take into consideration that if the family shelter had mostly children under five, they needed less food than the residents at the men's shelter, which wasn't feeding children.

I was calculating on my calculator under the table, figuring I could cut my piece of the pie.

At last, they turned to me and asked how much I needed.

I asked, "What would be left if Cocoon House went last?"

Bill said, "$750."

I said, "We'll go with $750."

Ed of Housing Hope, much more experienced than I, said, "You can't make it through a year on $750. What are you going to do?"

I said, "We'll take the $750 and buy a cow. It will last us."

I thought people's heads were going to explode. "Why the hell would you buy a cow?"

"I'm not buying a whole cow," I explained. "I'll buy a half a cow, butchered. The teens love hamburgers. Boeing volunteers donated a freezer to us. I can fill it with hamburger meat."

I thought about how well-stocked our refrigerator was every single day. Our grant money and donations went to food. Teenagers eat a lot of food. I would not depend on the federal food money; there wasn't enough to depend on. Food was a line item in every single grant I sent out.

The community regularly sent us donations. Almost all the donation money went to food.

When we were first opening, our licensor warned us, "You should lock up that fridge."

"Why?" I asked her.

"Kids will eat night and day. Get a big chain and put it around the fridge and lock it." She was serious. She was the licensor for our shelter. Whatever she told us we had to do, we were supposed to do.

"We are not locking the fridge. Don't put that requirement on my license."

"It's not a requirement, it's a suggestion. You'll see soon enough." She wrote something on her clipboard.

The teens were big eaters – and we sent someone to the store to restock as often as we needed.

Ed, who sat next to me in the meeting, smiled – then broke out laughing. He knew I'd never bought a cow or butchered one. It was just something I had heard about on the island. It was something people did in the rural farming community where I lived. I knew it would be the cheapest way to get something the teens at Cocoon would eat.

My cow went up on the whiteboard next to Cocoon.

The cow got us all thinking. Bill agreed to look into some basic items we all had to buy and see if he could purchase it in bulk through the food bank. We could share some of those items.

He asked us to shout out our items.

I yelled, "Ensure."

This raised questions from the group. Bill asked, "Why do you need Ensure? Isn't it that liquid shake for old people?"

"No one else is needing Ensure?" I was surprised. "Our kids are coming in starving. Sometimes they are too starved to eat food. We have to use Ensure first until they can start eating."

The room fell silent.

The horrors the homeless teens faced settled in around us. Our kids were suddenly no longer the extra mouths they had to feed.

At the end of the longest meeting my daughters ever had to sit through, I went over to pack up our things. My girls had long stopped coloring on the paper and had been drawing on the walls.

I looked at the Director of United Way and whispered, "I'll come back and fix it." I didn't want my daughters to think they had done anything wrong. They had been angels. The director assured me it was fine. He thought it cheered the place up.

It also made up my mind about one thing: that was Somer and Aliza's last meeting. It was not their last experience at Cocoon House. But it was just the last time I would ever ask them to wait while I was in a meeting. They were four years old. The writing was literally on the wall – it wasn't fair to them.

I thought of the other mommies on Whidbey Island, the ones who didn't work outside the home. They were making tomato sauce from the tomatoes they grew in their yards. They made the wooden toys their kids were using. Heck, one was still breastfeeding her four-year-old. Not something I could offer my daughters.

I didn't have other mommy friends that were running teen shelters. I was always filling someone's bowl. I just wanted to be sure Somer and Aliza were getting their bowls filled by me. I knew they weren't getting what the stay-at-home mommies were offering.

But did they need that? I didn't go to work on Thursday, Friday, Saturday and Sunday, but was that enough for my daughters? When they napped, I wrote grants. After bedtime, I called the shelter and checked in.

I felt like a butchered half-cow, dividing myself and trying to feed everyone. I worried that my daughters were having to share too much of their mom.

23

TRAY

Cocoon House wasn't a place full of hardened kids. "Hard kids" is a pretense – a form of prejudice. I always wondered if it was a way to deflect caring about kids who were without food or shelter. If they were "hard kids"– all of them, every single kid out there – then helping them, reaching them, was impossible. It was as if "hardened kids" deserved to be shut out of community. When I heard the words "hard kids," I thought, "Community failing."

The kids who came to Cocoon House taught us who they were. Some seemed hard on the outside. Some never did.

They could be cautious, slow to trust adults – and for good reason. All the kids came to us hungry. "Hungry kids" was a much better description. They were hungry for food, connection, relationship and so much more.

Most of the kids were anxious and sad. Hopeless. Beaten. Scared. Any of these words were more fitting than "hardened."

We took time to learn where the kids were from, who they had been connected to along the way. How did they lose their aunt, their grandma, their parent, their siblings? Where had they lived?

We didn't learn their stories all at once.

We took time. Kids chose which staff member they would want to spend some time around. A kid would follow one staff member around, sit by their side, interact. It became obvious who that kid had chosen. That was their person.

That would be the staff member who would learn their story. The one to take them to choose some clothes. The one who would check up on their medical needs and help them get into school.

We treated the kids gently. There were no negative comments about their hair, the body piercings they did themselves, the carvings on their skin, the black hoods and raincoats in the sunshine. We understood that these things were all the teens had.

They were covered in scars. Their clothes and hoods were like the shell of a tortoise: protection. We didn't tell them to stop dyeing their hair green or take out their piercings. We accepted them as they were.

Acceptance was something every kid needed. Some had been thrown out of their families because they were gay. Some had lost their parents to drugs and alcohol. All were losing themselves. Homelessness robs you of who you are, as if pieces of yourself fall away. You just don't matter to anyone. And some part of us needs to matter to someone.

Helping the kids meant letting them have some choice – who was the staff member they chose? What goals did they choose?

If they wanted to get a job, we would offer them help with clothes for job interviews. It was obvious which kids had been staying with us the longest. Over time, they shed the external "street look" and started wearing clothes that came in the donation bags often left on the porch of Cocoon House. Eventually, the kids took out the piercings on their own. The scars on their arms and legs, carved with razor blades, would heal.

The longer the teen stayed at Cocoon, the more of a transformation in appearance they underwent.

I guessed that as the kids felt safer, the choices of how they could "look" in the world changed. They were not trying to hide under a hood. They were not trying to look like a "hard kid" to keep people away. A kid named Levon once sculpted a self-portrait: a round ball of clay covered in nails.

Over and over, I watched the nails come off the clay for one kid after another. What was left was their soft insides.

And then there were those kids who never had hard nails on the outside.

Tray was one of those beautiful souls.

An African-American, Tray was a skinny kid who looked a bit young for his age. At 16, he came to the shelter after CPS took away his 3- and 4-year-old sisters. His mother was in jail, leaving Tray alone in an apartment caring for the little girls.

The landlord threw them out when Tray couldn't pay rent. Child Protective Services came and took the little girls to a foster home. But they did not take Tray. They had no place for him.

Tray was a still just a kid. A Black kid on the street in a largely white community, he could have been a target for white gang violence. Thankfully, he made it to Cocoon House.

He had one goal: to get his sisters back.

We did some research and learned his mom would be in jail for three to five years. Reuniting with his mother was not possible. We called his grandmother in Mississippi. She would take him in a heartbeat. She was 75 years old. We were happy to buy him a plane ticket to Mississippi. But there was one big problem. He refused to go. He would not leave Washington State without his sisters.

Okay. I couldn't just take his sisters out of foster care. I did understand that this was his goal, and it was reasonable to reunite him with his sisters and send them to Grandma as a family.

I contacted the Department of Social and Health Services to work on getting his sisters. After several months of roundabout phone calls inside the bureaucracy, we discovered a state-to-state agreement between Mississippi and Washington was needed in order to transfer the little girls.

And it turned out that Mississippi did not want to accept the girls because there was good chance that if Grandma didn't live, the girls would be in state care for their whole childhoods – an expense for the state. If Grandma did live, Mississippi would still need to provide some financial support to Grandma to help her raise the girls.

There was no deal the State of Mississippi would accept.

There was no deal Tray would accept. Tray would not leave Washington without them.

The Cocoon staff person Tray connected with was Tempel. They were a good match. Tray was calm and unshakeable. Tempel was a white Buddhist who practiced meditation. He was five years younger than me and wore knit hats, T-shirts and jeans. He was calm and soft, owned very few things and could see priorities clearly. He was a physics genius of sorts but tried to keep that hidden under his knit hat. Tempel was comfortable in the shelter, appreciated donations from the community and was a good listener.

Tempel tried to get Tray to look at his own life, separate from his vulnerable siblings. Tray was not in school and had a limited education. Tempel got him to work on his General Educational Development (GED) tests. This was a labor of love. Tempel bought a book to prepare for the GED and began the slow and patient work of preparing Tray for the high school equivalency test. There was a deep communion between the two. I watched them hunched over the GED prep book together, Tempel writing out practice math questions, and then passing the paper to Tray.

The GED must be passed within three tries. Tray was very smart. But he also had some trouble learning math – lots of trouble learning math. We wondered if he had sustained a head injury from beatings he took as a young boy.

Tray was honest and caring; he did the dishes, kept his room clean and asked if he could go to church on Sundays with a volunteer. He prayed. He was kind and helpful to other kids. He didn't smoke, he never did drugs or drank. In all ways, Tray was closer to God than anyone I had ever known.

On his first attempt, Tray didn't pass the GED.

Tempel rallied all kinds of help for Tray. He got him more qualified tutors, enrolled him in a program to help kids who were not in school. Tray hadn't intended to drop out. His mother had two little girls, and when they were born, he was afraid to leave them at home with her, so he stayed home from school to change diapers, make bottles and care for the babies. He couldn't go to school. He wouldn't leave the little girls alone with his mother and her "friends."

He was so far behind, and had such trouble learning math, it looked hopeless.

Tempel did not give up.

There were two things I looked for in people to work at Cocoon House: people who didn't give up, and people who could tolerate letting a kid be. Tempel was not a quitter, had great observation skills and was a math whiz. Every time Tempel was on shift, it was math time for Tray.

With my background as a teacher, I thought it was too much to ask of Tray. He was at a second- or third-grade level in math. The difficulty memorizing the times table and steps for each process made it harder for Tray. His memory was impaired. If he had been in school, he may have qualified for special education.

I shared what I knew as a teacher to help Tempel, being careful not to share how hopeless this path seemed. Tray had three shots to take the GED. Tempel was committed to giving it everything he had. Tray was committed to giving it everything he had. I shut my mouth and kept "what I knew as a teacher" to myself.

After much extra tutoring support, Tray failed his second attempt at the GED.

Hopelessness is a powerful contagion, and so is hope. I learned from working with kids that hope could triumph over anything. Tray had a lot to triumph over.

Without a high school diploma or GED, his whole life ahead looked bleak. He wasn't as concerned about his future as much as he was focused on his sisters. We arranged weekly visits with his sisters. Every Sunday, he would come down the steps of Cocoon in a white shirt and tie and wait for a family of strangers to pick him up and take him to church. After church, he got to visit for an hour with his sisters. That hour with his sisters helped get him through the rest of the week. Grief from being separated from his sisters was a pain he had to carry each day. There was nothing Tempel or I could do to make it better.

Tray needed to pass the GED to get jobs in the future. Tray needed to be reunited with his sisters. I had two states to convince this kid deserved better. He deserved the right to leave Washington and not be separated from his sisters, the two little ones he felt responsible for – the two little ones that were his family. He didn't have a mom and dad; he was the mom and dad.

24

SKYE

As a 34-year-old director, I was always faced with making choices about the money we had and where to spend it. My top financial priority was food. Feeding healthy foods to hungry teens was number one. Next came paying our beloved staff. The third priority was whatever seemed urgent at the time.

Nonprofits are sparse. If you can't manage on the thin resources, your nonprofit doors are shut.

I watched other nonprofits close and knew this could happen to Cocoon House at any time. We had nothing in savings. We survived on grants and donations that were only a few weeks ahead of the bills. Money was always on my mind. I didn't discuss the worry with anyone. It wasn't the staff's job to worry about money – they had plenty of other things to do. I saw it as mine alone.

Louisa, who I always thought of as "the hat lady," ran the local drug-and-alcohol treatment agency. To look at her, you would never know Louisa ran a nonprofit. She dressed up every day in a dress, heels and a hat that matched her dress. I ran around in black jeans, sneakers and a button-down Oxford shirt. A look that seemed clean, but simple. It was a look my roommate had in college, and I thought it was timeless. Fifteen years later, I was still in the same look.

As I got to know Louisa, I learned she'd had a sad childhood, moving from foster home to foster home. How she dressed was for her a way of "having" – covering up the dirt of her childhood with something that made her feel valuable. The hats made her feel exceptional.

When Louisa's agency could no longer make it financially, she called me. She was losing her building, her staff, all the furniture and the nonprofit.

"Come take whatever you want out of here before I lock the doors," she said. "At least I will know all my stuff went somewhere good."

My heart sank, but I went. This is what I feared every day: shutting our doors. I entered what was once a busy agency, now quiet, the phones no longer ringing. I looked around at the empty desks pushed to the middle of the room, boxes piled up along the wall. Louisa stood in heels, a pale pink skirt, tailored suit jacket and a small hat with birdcage netting over her forehead.

"Go through the boxes. Take whatever you want."

I found phones, unplugged, with the wires hanging off the back. "Can I have the phone system?"

She looked at me, stunned. "You don't have a phone system?"

"No."

I felt embarrassed.

"I don't want to tell you how much that cost me," she said. "Go ahead, take it."

I handed her a piece of paper.

"One more thing. Write down the best drug-and-alcohol counselor you have. Give me their number. I'll hire them." Louisa took the paper and wrote one name.

This is how I got one of the most incredible human beings who ever worked with teens: KarenAnn, a large white woman, who had a smoker's cough and a wheeze, and was at least 25 years older than me. Like many drug counselors, she was also in recovery. Her reputation was well known in the youth-service field in Washington State. I called her and invited her to meet me at Cocoon. She walked in and sat down in a chair, wheezing a bit. She had on brown polyester pants, sensible flat shoes and a striped short-sleeved blouse.

KarenAnn was expecting an interview for the job, but I only had one question, "When can you start?"

KarenAnn had a following. One member of her following was a 22-year-old named Skye. Karen Ann brought Skye in to meet me.

He was wearing roller skates. She said, "He needs a job." I asked the obvious question, given that I'd just hired her from a drug alcohol agency: "Is he clean?"

"Yes."

Skye had pale white skin and long blue hair. Whizzing past on roller skates, he reminded me of a crow.

When we met in the Cocoon House living room, I said, "You can leave the skates outside."

He stood up, circled for me like he was on an ice rink, and said, "I need to keep my skates on."

I was desperate for good staff, so I hired Skye-on-skates on a trial basis.

Skye was warm and talkative with the teens. He wasn't sexual or provocative toward anyone. This was an important safety issue around our teens. He was contained to himself and his skates, yet he was friendly and open. He came to work in the same torn jeans and T-shirt. I had the sense that he didn't have a lot of things. He never asked what I would pay him, or how many hours he had to work. He didn't wear a watch. He was often late.

I asked him if he could work on getting to the shelter on time. He explained he took three buses. He lived very far out at the county line, near the state prison, and slept in a van. He didn't drive the van or have a driver's license. He depended on buses, and those were very unreliable in the rural part of the county. He explained that to get to the shelter on time, the bus would get him there two hours early. The only other bus would get him to us 15 minutes late, if things ran on time.

As I listened to the distance he was willing to go to get to us, I rethought how important it was that he get there on time. The kids adored him. He was an assistant on his shift. There was always someone else, one of our more experienced staff, and they could handle the shelter for 15 or 30 minutes without him.

Skye seemed to love his job. He stayed late. He was always first to offer to cover someone's shift. He didn't know how to cook, but he learned from the farmer, the Buddhist and the doctor.

On one of his shifts at the shelter, he called me at home and said the other staff on duty never made it in and a snowstorm was coming.

"When?"

"Look out your window." I don't know how I'd managed not to notice this; my daughters and I were making art out of shaving cream.

"Skye, how is it in Everett?"

"Everything is covered, and the snow warning is for feet, not inches." I thought of the van he was living in.

"Skye, please stay at the shelter, I don't know if any buses will run."

He agreed to stay. For the first time, Skye would be on shift alone. Not ideal. I said, "Skye, call me every hour."

The ferry boats to get off the island were stopped for the night. I had no way to get to the shelter. I looked at a map and noted where each of our staff lived. No one was close to the shelter. I couldn't ask anyone to drive in. It would have to be Skye alone.

"Skye, promise to keep calling me. Is it warm in the house? Check the fridge. How much food is there?" He listed every item to me on every shelf. "Skye, cook up the chicken now, in case the power goes out overnight." Our area has frequent power outages with high winds. With snow too, we could be out for days.

Every hour, on the hour, the guy who didn't wear a watch called me.

The kids were sleeping. It was a quiet night. The chicken was cooked. The power stayed on.

Skye stayed awake all night.

By morning the whole Seattle region was snowed in. No cars were allowed on roads. There were strong wind gusts and more snow.

I called Skye and explained that I needed him to stay. I realized he had been awake for 24 hours.

"Skye, I can't get anyone to you."

When the teens woke up, it was playtime with Skye. He played cards, made snow angels in the yard with the kids. But none of the kids had snow boots, so they quickly went back in the house to stay dry. Skye sounded fresh and alert.

That night I asked Skye to sleep on the couch. "Don't call me every hour. Sleep. You need sleep."

Skye held the shelter together, kept the food going and entertained the kids for four straight days.

He was no longer my junior staff. After the snowstorm, he became one of our rock-star staff.

And he always wore his skates in the house.

The kids saw alternative ways of being from every staff member. From the farmer, they learned to plant a garden. From Tempel, they learned about meditation. From Skye, they learned about music and moving around on skates. From Kim and Danny, they got everything else: how to work a washing machine, which bus to take to school, how to check for fevers, new sneakers that fit to replace ones with holes, homework help. It all added up to the care and attention everyone needed.

I watched all our staff members grow, developing their abilities. They were becoming not only valuable to Cocoon House, but to the whole community. When staff members left Cocoon for other jobs, they left as flexible, creative problem-solvers, able to keep hope going wherever it was needed. Saying you worked at Cocoon House meant something to other nonprofits, to city and county governments. The team I worked with included the most capable people with whom I have ever worked. There was no room for any of us to drop the ball. The consequences of us failing in any way meant the only teen shelter in the community would be closed. We all understood we had to keep the place open; there was no alternative.

25

PRISON

Participating in community meant I attended many meetings on behalf of Cocoon House: some by choice, some because I had to and some that I had to organize myself. In each meeting I had to figure out how to belong.

For my job, I needed to attend the statewide task force, a network of youth-service agencies, the committee of adult and family shelters, and meetings of the board of directors for Cocoon House. In each group, I had to patch the wounds I carried from childhood, the wounds of not belonging.

Inside, I always felt like an outsider. The outsider status was a legacy of my childhood, and though I belonged and had a community and a family, an outsider lived inside me. I knew her like I knew my name.

The pink house where I'd grown up was in a middle-class neighborhood of mostly white Jewish families. All the kids in my neighborhood lived with their parents. Grammy and Poppy had a place in Brooklyn where they spent all their weekdays, usually until after dinnertime. They hired housekeepers to take care of me and Adam.

So, I felt I was standing on the outside, watching the neighbors' families be families. I was invited to join them for dinner and adventures. When I did, I knew I was getting something from my friends' families that my own didn't possess and couldn't give me.

I learned how to belong to other families. But I was never a full member. Outsider status felt like a permanent state, like something that should have been listed on my driver's license and passport.

Kids who are homeless are also outsiders. At my first Rotary Club meeting, someone leaned over my shoulder and said, "Your Cocoon kids are just a bunch of moths." That didn't hurt as much as it could have. Outsider status was where we belonged. Cocoon kids were living on the edge of everything.

But the necessary work of Cocoon House meant we couldn't remain outsiders. It was my job to embed our program in the community. I had to move from the familiar outsider zone to the insider zone. California Ted taught me how important it was to make allies.

Giving "talks" as a guest speaker was the way I introduced Cocoon House to community members. I gave 20-minute talks wherever I was invited: a bowling alley, a conference meeting, a motorcycle club, an attorney's lunch group. When I was invited to speak to the local Rotary Club, I came back to the words about the kids being moths. So, I thought I'd try and have the Rotarians feel the experience of the moths and understand their outsider stories. I grabbed a handful of my daughters' dolls. I wasn't sure how the Beanie Babies, the troll dolls, or Hoppy and Muffy would go over in a room full of Rotarians with suits and ties, or heels and expensive handbags.

The Rotary group met at The Everett Yacht Club, glass windows overlooking boats and the water. The Rotarians met at noon. They were all leaders, trailblazers, successful entrepreneurs, people who had worked hard to earn their standing in the community.

In my mind, they were people who were hard to impress.

I walked onto the stage with my collection of dolls in a wicker basket. My clothes and basket signaled I was an outsider. I felt the sting of being an outsider from the top of my head down through my toes. Goose bumps covered my arms. I didn't belong on this stage.

But I looked out over the audience and saw California Ted and Tim the Boeing engineer who volunteered to make the shelter repairs every month. Their eyes were warm and encouraging. I took a breath, exhaled slowly like I did when I swam, and then held up each of the dolls and, one by one, told their stories.

Muffy, Hoppy, the Beanie Babies and troll dolls became the kids staying at Cocoon House.

I told some of the challenges the dolls had experienced: a parent in jail, a parent who'd killed themselves, a parent who threw Hoppy out at age 15 because he was gay. I then got off the stage and handed my dolls to a group of Rotarians at a table. I had them get up and move the dolls around the room as I told the story of how the dolls moved from place to place until they ran out of places and landed at Cocoon House.

The "dolly presentation" broke open the hearts in the room. The Rotarians could feel what the struggle was for each of the Cocoon kids. Some Rotarians had been foster parents, some had their own struggles and recovery with addiction, some had felt like outsiders their whole lives.

The line between outsider and insider melted.

A few days after the dolly presentation, Tim, my volunteer handyman, invited me to become a member of the Rotary Club. And just that quickly, my outsider status returned. The Rotary members in the yacht club had an air of wealth around them. I was not running an airplane company or an engineering firm. I didn't own a bank or a restaurant or a successful medical practice. I felt small, inadequate.

I joined the group for the Cocoon kids. I joined because the Cocoon kids needed me to gather more supporters. But I struggled with not feeling like I was "enough" to be a Rotarian.

Each Tuesday, I set aside my feelings and found my way into the lunchtime banter. I found my way to making some friends in the room. I got used to not having the wealth or connections they had, but knew there was more than that to Rotary. Cocoon House was part of their community. Cocoon House was not a place of wealth or expensive clothes. Each Tuesday I had to sit in my car in the parking lot and repeat a little mantra to myself before going into the Rotary meeting: "I am not an outsider. I am a member."

But feeling like an outsider stayed with me. That's why I agreed to accept the next speaking engagement.

I sat at the kitchen table, opening the Christmas mail. This was before the internet, when people wrote handwritten notes to Cocoon

House, enclosing $5 from a lemonade stand, $100 from someone who sent blessings with the money. I liked the idea of someone sending a blessing by mail.

Then there were cards and checks from my childhood friends. I was a long way from New York, yet my closest friends and their parents thought about Cocoon House. At the holidays, Cocoon was on their donation list. Their letters were personal. They knew me. They asked about my daughters. They let me know they were proud of me. Only they'd known me as a child and teen. Only they truly understood how Cocoon House was the effort of a young girl who hadn't had much. These notes and cards were from the people who'd watched over me when I needed them. They were my stand-in family – my cocoon, before there was a Cocoon House.

I read and reread their notes and stuffed them in my purse, talismans. Once those were removed from the pile, I continued opening envelopes. One of my favorite things was reading letters sent to Cocoon House at Christmas.

The local corner fruit stand, the 25th Street Market, donated a year of fresh fruit weekly. I could go by and pick up a bag of whatever we needed. That brought tears to my eyes. A full year! They understood that we needed to feed kids every day, not just at Christmas. Their letter had a stamped address for the fruit stand. They'd stamped it again and again on their card.

Then, there was an envelope, no return address, no name.

I pulled from the white, small envelope a piece of loose-leaf paper, blue lines on white paper like I used in school as a child. The letter, written in pencil, started apologetically.

Sarri,

You may not want to hear from us. But we sat down together to write you a letter. We have a gift for you. All of us have been working on a project to raise money in the prison for Cocoon House. If we had a place like Cocoon House when we were growing up, we never would have ended up in here.

Most of us came from really bad homes, not really homes at all.

Thank you for making this shelter for kids.

We want you to know we are watching over this shelter.

We are asking one thing: Would you please come to see us to pick up the check? We have $500 for Cocoon House.
   Signed,
   The Lifers at Washington State Prison, Monroe

I read the letter again. Then I read it aloud to the staff on shift.

"What are you going to do?" Kim, the gutsy social worker, asked.

"I'm going to call the prison and check it out. If this is real, I'm going to go see them. Who is going with me?"

Tempel pushed his chair back from the table. The farmer looked at the floor. Luke whistled.

Mr. Calm Danny nodded yes. I looked at him and said, "It's you and me."

I called the prison and spoke to a deputy and confirmed that the "lifers" – sentenced to life in prison with no hope of parole – had adopted Cocoon House. They were earning money each day for labor they did in the prison. The men had pooled their earnings and given it to Cocoon House. I couldn't imagine six men working all year to save up $500 with no chance of leaving prison. No hope for themselves, and they were thinking of us.

I asked for permission to come see them and thank them.

The director of the prison told me the long list of rules about visiting the prison – and an even longer list to visit the lifers.

Danny and I showed up at the prison on our assigned date, after dinner on a weeknight, long after sunset had given way to nightfall. The darkness outside made the visit feel ominous.

The prison was enormous and looked like a foreboding castle. It was the second-largest prison in Washington State and housed over 2,500 men.

As we entered the prison, we were searched. They touched down our legs, across my breasts. It was humiliating. The doors were locked behind us, and my stomach dropped 20 feet. We were locked in. We went through three more doors and corridors, each one locking behind us with a heavy thud.

I felt myself go pale.

"Why am I here?" I thought.

I couldn't answer the question. They could have mailed the $500. I didn't personally visit every donor. What was I thinking?

Maybe I was thinking about my father. He was in prison when I was a teenager. Maybe I was trying to visit him. The idea of locking myself into a prison now felt insane. I was feeling waves of panic and claustrophobia, like being stuck in an elevator that has stopped moving. The ceiling was low, the locked bars were behind us. No way out.

Danny read my mind.

"We'll be out of here soon."

A guard led us into a room outside where the lifers were waiting. I could see them through thick glass windows.

"Before you go in," he said, "you need to know they run this place. They are in for life. They have nothing to lose. I can't protect you in there. They are very excited you are visiting, but excitement here can sometimes lead to bad things."

My panic was growing. My ears were burning as he went on.

The guard explained, "Try to stay calm. Go up against a wall and crouch into a tight ball if anything goes wrong."

My assistant looked at me. He smiled and said, "Isn't this a great idea?"

Laughter helped. The guard opened the door.

I looked around the room. There were eight of them and two of us. All the men were seated.

They seemed young, with black hair. Most were white; one older man had graying hair and was Black. He smiled at me. I took a breath. I didn't want to think about how he and the others ended up as lifers.

"Hi. I came to thank you." I looked around the room. One of the young-looking men was crying.

I wasn't sure what to say next. I thought of how many years they had in front of them. They were dressed in the same faded jumpsuits.

I asked them if there was anything they wanted to talk about in our time together.

One guy called out, "Tell us about the shelter. Tell us the story of how it started."

I asked, "Did you read about it in the paper?" Their heads nodded.

"But we want to hear the story from you," one man said.

Suddenly, the eight men felt like eight little boys who wanted me to tell them a story they had heard a million times.

So, I told them about the Lions club, the bingo parlor and how we started Cocoon House. I had brought them photos of the shelter, and they came closer to look at the pictures. My assistant's eyes flashed at me. He took one slow step back. He was reminding me of where we were.

I told them to keep the pictures as a thank-you.

A guard watching from the booth above the room signaled me our visit was over. I thanked the men who seemed so young. I couldn't think about what else to say while leaving a room I knew they would never leave. One of them stepped forward and said, "We're watching over Cocoon House. No one is going to mess with you." I wasn't sure what to say to that. I nodded.

Each door slammed with a thud as we left. Though we were outside and in the parking lot, I didn't feel free. Some part of me felt confused. Like, what separated those men from the kids in the shelter? The Cocoon kids were trapped in homelessness. Tray and Lilly with baby Will had no way out either.

I could never imagine what it felt like to be a lifer. Many people couldn't imagine what it felt like to be a teen who was homeless and without a loving family.

26

SHELTER IS NOT ENOUGH

I had been running the shelter for three years. We'd become competent at working with kids who were living outside of families and schools. Cocoon became a place between nowhere and somewhere. We started to understand the rule: bodies first. We got used to kids coming to us sick. Now, we started by checking for fevers, infections, aches and wounds. Then food. Then showering, getting lice out of their hair and getting them into clean clothes. Last, getting the knots and grease out of hair that stuck to itself like glue. Their bodies.

That first step from nowhere to somewhere was often one of looking at the piles of donated clothes and choosing something to wear. It was Christmas to the kids. Having. Receiving. Choosing. There isn't anything to have or choose in nowhere.

As soon as possible, each kid was taken back to school. Each kid had a different school plan based on where they left off. We got kids into GED test programs, high school equivalency programs, alternative schools, half-day schools – wherever they would be accepted and were willing to try.

Some kids were taken back home by their families. Some kids were taken in by aunts, uncles, grandmas, older brothers and sisters. Some kids had no place to go back to. Not anywhere. Those kids stayed on at Cocoon. Cocoon house for them was no longer a shelter; it became home. Lilly and baby Will, Tray and a few others became long-term residents.

One day Jim, my guardian angel from the Lions Club, stopped by. I offered him coffee as usual. He turned down the coffee, saying, "Let's go for a walk."

I grabbed my sweater.

Jim wanted to know how the shelter was doing. He was concerned about those kids who were living permanently in the shelter. I was concerned too. It was like living in a train station, with new kids coming and going. The residents were exposed to sick kids and lice over and over.

And they were like junior staff, taking care of the new kids who would have trouble sleeping.

Often, new kids were anxious or depressed.

We were a block away from the shelter house when Jim stopped walking and said, "That's why you need a bigger building. The need for Cocoon House is big. The place is always full. Those kids can't grow up in a shelter. They need a place to grow up." I agreed, but I had no vision of how to make that happen. I had spent three years learning how to get kids from nowhere to somewhere. I spent three years making partnerships with schools, counseling programs, teen parent programs, drug-and-alcohol treatment programs. Three years getting food stamps and Medicaid for teens, access to routine health care and hospitalization for emergencies, dental care for emergencies. Three years begging for services for underage kids when there was no guardian to sign consent forms. We didn't have a single dime to buy those services.

Every service had to be negotiated for free.

All our money was spent on bills to run the shelter, pay staff, buy food, keep the house stocked with needed supplies. I was writing grants all the time. Local funders didn't have a line item in their budget for teen shelters. I had to educate the funders about how it worked and what we needed.

I thought back to my very first grant with the Boeing Employees Community Fund. I had written a grant application. A few months went by, and they said they were ready to review my grant application. They came to the shelter with six members of their board. We sat at the kitchen table. We couldn't close the shelter for a meeting, so every now and then a teen would pop into the kitchen to grab some food.

Tim was the leader of the Boeing employees. He wanted to see our budget, accounting records and receipts. I was prepared.

I passed him my blue loose-leaf notebook and shoebox. The receipts are all stapled and labeled in envelopes in the shoe box. The budget was written by hand in the notebook, and pages of revisions to and monthly notes on the budget were organized by date from the day we opened.

Tim's jaw dropped. Then he burst out laughing. He said he had never seen anything like this in a nonprofit. Obviously, I'd impressed him with my impeccable record-keeping. Later, of course, I learned that was not what he meant. But the very next day, after the Boeing team left, a big surprise arrived at the Cocoon House doorstep. A freezer! A place to store more food for the kids – the freezer for the cow.

And that freezer was followed with a $50,000 check.

Now, Jim of the Lions Club thought that, with my drop of grant-writing experience, I could expand the program. He was nuts. I had not a second of time to even think about it.

"Look around you," he said, standing on the sidewalk in downtown Everett. "What do you see?"

"I see an old motel, a Chinese restaurant and a Denny's restaurant."

"That motel. Let's go look around."

"It looks abandoned, Jim."

"It is, kind of."

We walked around the motel. There were wires stripping power from somewhere. Empty beer cans. A guy sleeping on the second floor outside a door. He was homeless. He woke up startled and asked us what the hell we were doing there.

"She owns this building," Jim said. "We are looking around." He pulled keys from his pocket and jingled them in the air.

"Jim, that's funny – I own the place."

He looked at me and dropped the keys in my hand.

"Yes, you own this."

"What the heck?"

Jim started laughing. "We mortgaged the bingo parlor and bought you this 30-unit motel. Now you just need to find about a million dollars to renovate it and make more housing for those kids."

My first words as I looked at the cream-colored mammoth building were, "Jim, I can't! You'll lose your bingo parlor! I don't know how to raise a million dollars!"

My mouth went dry; my stomach heaved. I thought I would vomit on my shoes.

Jim put his hand on my shoulder. "Look me in the eye."

I looked at his eyes.

"Yes, you can. You just haven't done it yet. But you can do this. All of us Lions know you can do this. Trust me. We know you can do this."

I thought, "Damn this town." I was surrounded by Pacific Northwesterners with a can-do attitude. The Everett Lions believed I was one of them, in a town where Bill Boeing built airplanes, Bill Gates built Microsoft, and Fred Hutchinson Cancer Research Center developed bone marrow transplants and mini-transplants using stem cells. Dr. Scribner at The University of Washington figured out how to deliver dialysis through the arm. The list of discoveries and firsts is impressive. The Pacific Northwest was filled with people who invented things, built things from scratch, cleverly devised solutions and then gave them to the world. This part of the country had a can-do, let's-make-it-ourselves attitude about everything. Figuring things out was as common as rain.

The Lions had mistaken me for a Pacific Northwesterner blood and bone, someone that just could create solutions. The Lions owned our shelter house. And now they had mortgaged everything they had for Cocoon House to expand. They put all their eggs in one basket. My basket. They were all more experienced and wiser than me. They knew better than to invest everything they had in one place. What the hell were they thinking?

"What if I fail?" I asked Jim.

"You won't."

He left me standing there with the keys in my hand.

27

A WHOLE NEW BUILDING

The 30-unit motel had four drunk, white Vietnam veterans in residence. They met me at the door with their guns strapped across their shoulders. I brought them coffee and donuts and sat on the cement with them, ignoring the smell of urine that was either coming from one of the men or the puddle near me. I explained the building was going to be fixed up for kids who had no place to go. The veterans wanted to stay. The "abandoned" building was their home too.

They followed me as I went from room to room of the 30 units, making notes on all the needed rehabilitation. I got to one room and found pictures of me from the newspaper pinned to the walls and scattered on the floor. The four veterans had used this room for target practice.

I called the Veterans Assistance program and asked them to come down and help get the guys into some other housing. They had been squatting in this cold building. They'd rigged up electricity by running wires all over the outside from a pole up the street. The toilets were growing mold.

Each time I visited the building, I left shaking. I didn't know how to get building rehabilitation grants. I had gotten the shelter by writing my request on a napkin and appearing in a bingo hall. Grants to renovate a building were different from operating grant funds. I would need to seek money from new sources. The 30-unit motel was a new building that had never opened. It was built without permits. Squatters and abandonment had turned it into a place of despair.

I didn't know if the veterans would ever get housing somewhere else. I didn't know if they would just shoot me in the back one day. I didn't know how much it would cost to operate and staff a building of that size.

I couldn't get the state licensing department to discuss it. The place was uninhabitable. It wouldn't be enough to show the building to a licensor and explain how it "could" look one day.

Bureaucrats, as I had come to know them, had no imagination. I was afraid to send out grant requests. The funders would ask me questions about long-term funding that I had no idea how to answer.

I had to figure all this out before I could ask anyone for help.

I felt too young to be handed this enormous building. My skills were inadequate. But the motel couldn't just be returned to the Lions Club. The teens coming to Cocoon House needed more than shelter. They needed a place to grow up. We were turning new kids away who needed shelter because we were always full. Jim and the other Lions were right. We needed more room.

Each day I walked from the shelter to the abandoned motel, chewing on questions. I returned without answers to the shelter, looked at the kids' faces and convinced myself that I couldn't give up.

Not giving up was something we talked about every day in Cocoon House. Not giving up was something we breathed in and out. As a staff, we wouldn't give up on a kid. As the executive director, I would not give up on finding the resources we needed. The teens could not give up either. We were all together tied by one promise – we wouldn't give up.

So, I went in the only direction I knew how to go: forward, looking for people who could help me learn how to do what needed doing.

I had to move from the kids' table to the grown-up table. I had to move away from the poorly funded youth programs, where my friend California Ted was watching my back, and go to meetings with the poorly funded adult housing providers. The housing programs for adults knew how to access money to build long-term housing.

Of course, they didn't want another mouth to feed at their funding table. But they also could see that the kids at Cocoon House needed more. The adult shelters didn't want to get into all the liability issues of housing kids, so they made room for me at their funding tables. They invited me to take scraps. Whatever money wasn't needed by all the other housing programs would be pushed my way. I watched. I learned. Like a puppy at the heels of the big dog, I took what I could get.

But Cocoon House couldn't grow on table scraps. I had to find another way. I went directly to the funders to convince them to make room for Cocoon House in their budgets.

I went to our local United Way and asked how much they thought Cocoon House could reasonably hope for? The answer was $15,000. After all the other agencies got their funding, this is what would be left. And all the others were receiving more.

If Cocoon House was going to have long-term housing, we needed more money. So instead of applying for $15,000, I applied for what we needed: $65,000. The CEO of the United Way called me.

"What the hell are you doing?"

I said I was applying for what the kids needed to have a housing program. He warned I would be turned down and that I should have asked for the $15,000 that would be almost a guarantee.

"What if you get nothing?" he asked.

"If we got $15,000, we wouldn't be open for long, so it would be the same as nothing."

It was hard to say those words to him.

But there was some truth about nothing – about homelessness and children – that we needed to face as a community. Did they want us there or not? We couldn't be outsiders at the local funding tables.

The community volunteers reviewing grants for United Way awarded Cocoon House the full $65,000.

I learned from this that I had to push for what the kids needed, and I could not sit quietly. I had to get a space for them in everyone's budget.

We secured state funds to rehabilitate the motel. It would be a million-dollar renovation. The county and city each had some money in the rehabilitation budget as well.

I signed papers at the county courthouse: a covenant, that if Cocoon House closed as an organization, the building would continue to serve homeless youth. The land itself was secured for the future. The covenant meant kids with no place to go would always have a place in Everett.

The building changed Cocoon residents' status from outsiders to insiders – for good. We had investors in our home from the state, the city and the county.

Though Cocoon was gaining on insider status, my personal status hadn't changed much.

No one felt comfortable with me overseeing the million-dollar renovation of the new building: not the state, not the county, not the city, not my own board of directors. The Cocoon board wanted to get a volunteer to oversee the construction through the Boeing loaned-executives program.

Every funding entity appointed someone to oversee construction – there was a strong team in place. They oversaw every aspect, from design to hiring the contractor to overseeing each payment on construction.

I was sidelined. I got to watch, nod my head "yes" and ask questions of the team.

A year later, construction was finished, and we were ready to open. I had party hats and the furniture moved in. The kids were claiming their rooms, running around the new building, shouting to each other across the new outdoor courtyard. Our Boeing loaned-executive waved me over to meet someone, the fire inspector. I walked across the muddy courtyard.

"Damn. When are we getting grass?"

"Um, we have much bigger problems than grass," the loaned executive said. "We can't pass the fire inspection."

"What do we need?" I asked the fire inspector. Surely this was a solvable problem.

"You need a goddamn sprinkler system throughout this building." He shook his head. "You need to clear everyone off this site till you can pass inspection." He thumped his hand on the wall, tucked his clipboard under his arm and walked out the door.

I looked at the loaned executive.

"How big of a problem is this?"

"Oh, it's big." He got tears in his eyes. "I don't know how we all missed this." He looked out at the 30-unit motel, new paint, new windows, the new kitchen and lodge, and he shook his head.

All the experts, from architects to contractors to the loaned executive, didn't realize we needed a sprinkler system?

How big of a problem was this? Gigantic. It would cost $75,000 we didn't have.

By now, I had learned a lot about grants and funders. I had come a long way from the days of writing a request on a napkin, or submitting a grant in pencil. I knew that no funder anywhere would pay for a problem after the fact. They awarded grants in advance. You proposed the idea.

You didn't make a mistake and then ask the funders to pay for it. Grants didn't pay for mistakes.

I had no funding source to turn to. I took home the budget pages from the committee of brilliant experts and cried over them. I looked at every line over and over. Until something hit me: a line item in the budget to pay the state taxes on new construction. It was $40,000.

I called the contractor.

"Have we paid those taxes yet?"

"No."

"Okay, don't pay them."

I was no longer on the sidelines.

I called the Seth, the prosecutor, who was in the room when I proposed Cocoon House to the Lions. "How could we get out of paying state taxes on construction?"

He put me in touch with our state representative, Jeri Costa. Overnight, she came up with a bill that said construction of youth emergency housing could be done tax free. Jeri ran all over our state capital with that bill, like a marathoner running for first place. She got the sponsorship, she got the votes, and she got that bill through. It solved half the problem: It saved us $40,000 in taxes – about half of what we needed.

I had no place left for fear.

I had gone through every fear. Like crying when you are all out of tears, I had no more room for fear.

Fear could watch as I did what I had to do. It could come along and watch as I ran a teen shelter that needed money pumped into it every single day.

It could watch as I opened a second building for homeless kids.

Fear would not help me.

People who met me in my role as a nonprofit director thought I was fearless. That wasn't true. I was numbing it. Not with drugs or alcohol – I was numbing it with defiance. I couldn't do fear and keep going. It was one or the other.

Defiance was always ready. I let her take the wheel. Tank Girl emerged. Though I have no actual military experience, I pictured this part of myself riding around in an armored truck, wearing the green army pants of my adolescence, the ones with the strawberry patch on the butt.

As the problems around me grew larger, out came the part of me that was strong enough to handle these issues. I trusted Tank Girl.

28

MANY CHANGES

Tank Girl wasn't suited for everything in my life. She was a small piece of me. The mommy part of me was softer and growing with my daughters.

As my daughters turned four and a half years old, life was shifting. They were starting kindergarten. Somer insisted on learning to tie her shoes before going to kindergarten. She saw older kids could tie their shoes and wouldn't go to school until she could tie her own. Together we sat making rabbit ears a hundred times.

There is urgency to some of the strangest things as a mom. One day your kids are guided by what you offer; the next minute they have ideas of their own, and you are running behind them, trying to keep up.

I thought about what I wanted for them in their "school years." I wanted to be the mommy that picked them up from school each day, gave them afternoon snacks, listened to their stories, attended their field trips, volunteered in their classrooms. I wanted to be present every day when school let out. These were my shoes to tie. I was more like the spaghetti-sauce-making moms than anyone imagined. I wanted to be home for my daughters.

This idea of being a mom that picked up her kids each day was something I would not sacrifice for Cocoon House. Even as I was lying awake at night, trying to come up with funding for a sprinkler system or open a new building, I knew I couldn't expect myself to be all that Cocoon needed.

Cocoon's needs could be met by a well-developed staff team. I saw my role shifting at Cocoon House – and a firm boundary forming that would not allow Cocoon House to take all my time away from being a mom.

Below the surface of the mommy-who-works circus, there was something else happening that was much more difficult to find my way through, needs in my home I couldn't fix. My marriage was ending.

It was a culmination of many things that broke us. No one can ever look at a marriage and dissect it down to one or two things. When people divorce, it's always many things. Too many things. Too many broken things.

Somewhere inside of me, there was a small child, the same age as Somer and Aliza, who ached for me to tend to her.

She was frozen in time in a terrible courtroom where she lost her parents, her home and parts of her family. I had to give that little girl inside of me a home too.

Seeing Somer and Aliza at that same age made me aware of how responsible and alone I felt at their age.

I came face to face with my vulnerability as they turned four.

I needed tenderness. I needed to heal the little girl inside of me. I needed a home that was safe, peaceful and comforting to four-year-olds, and where I felt loved.

I allowed myself to feel the grief of losing my marriage. Losing a family. I was not just losing my husband. I was losing something I wanted for my daughters: a family that was whole.

My head was always hurting after the divorce. I walked around with an ice bag on my head. Ice was the only thing that helped me cope with the throbbing physical pain of being separated from my husband.

In time I could recover from what I lost, but the grief for what my daughters had lost would always be with me. I knew this hurt them.

I covered my knowledge with puppet shows, art, dance and playing games, and by doing all things four-year-old-ish, but inside I carried their broken hearts. The divorce hurt my daughters in ways no parent ever wants to hurt their kids. Spaghetti-sauce-making moms don't hurt their kids like this. I wish the marriage had been a better place of belonging and home for all of us. But it wasn't.

My divorce changed my feeling of responsibility. I had no financial backup for me and my girls. I had to think about every expense. To the financial worries of Cocoon House, I now added my own financial worries. My ex-husband and I shared custody and lived within a few miles of one another. I took on extra jobs when my daughters were with their dad to be sure there was enough money. I was too proud to admit we couldn't make it on my salary from Cocoon House.

I had learned frugality at Cocoon House, and being careful with money helped me in our new life. I made sandwiches to carry with us, but we still went out on day trips. I bought everything on sale. I bought us a 700-square-foot farmhouse that came with a blind horse and five acres. I rehomed the horse, got bunk beds for my daughters and set up a new home. I wallpapered the kitchen in joyful vegetables. We used art supplies at the kitchen table with the sun pouring down on us. It was as cozy as the mouse house of George and Matilda.

My Cocoon hours flipped to the hours Somer and Aliza were in school. Fridays became my holy days. I didn't do any work for Cocoon on Fridays. I used this day to go into my daughters' classrooms and volunteer. I did errands. I made spaghetti sauce.

My relationship to Cocoon House changed after my divorce. Cocoon was always described by others as a child of mine. But I had never thought of Cocoon as my child. I thought of it as something that grew from my imagination. It grew from an idea. Cocoon was important to me, but I always understood that its existence was tenuous, dependent on funders. With funding, Cocoon's needs would someday be met by the many people who worked there.

My new goal was to make Cocoon House strong enough for me to one day leave and let others run it.

But at this time, neither Cocoon nor I was strong enough yet for me to leave. If I'd left then, no one would have put into it the sweat and attention needed to keep its doors open. It was a demanding thing to carry, but I knew it was mine.

Carrying my daughters was lighter. Easier. Joyful and full of love.

Cocoon was harder to carry. It wasn't easy. Cocoon was always a mixture of many feelings.

But inside of that complexity, I found so much joy.

It would be six more years before I felt I could leave. I didn't tell anyone that my goal was to make Cocoon House strong enough to weather anything without me. But having this as my goal changed the way I did things. I thought about the skills every staff person needed to thrive without me. I thought about what the board needed to know to make decisions on their own. I thought about how to let others steer Cocoon House. And I calculated what Cocoon would need financially to survive a leadership transition. Sustainability became my goal for Cocoon House.

How could I make sure Cocoon House would always be there for kids?

29

THE ONE-TWO PUNCH

I'd felt stretched very thin finding all the resources for teens at Cocoon House. And the new building was requiring more – more problems to solve, from the sprinkler system to licensing to funding.

It was clear why the new building was needed. In the shelter, we were short-term, temporary. If kids stayed longer, we tried to become what they needed, but we were a shelter and therefore fundamentally unsuited to longer-term housing. New needs – and new problems – were bound to be part of opening the new building.

In addition, there was the job of advocacy. I wasn't trained as an advocate; I wasn't trained as a social worker. Advocacy came intuitively. I was a beginner, learning by doing, making mistakes. My advocacy experience was limited to the streets of Everett.

I didn't know I had to monitor the state capitol at all times. It felt like a surprise attack when the Division of Child and Youth Services created a youth shelter license for the State of Washington.

I called other homeless teen advocates around the state to see if anyone in any corner of Washington understood why this was suddenly coming up. Every advocate I spoke to – people who ran drop-in centers, people who did needle exchanges, people who ran feeding programs, teen parent groups, group homes for teens – had had no awareness that this was coming.

"Any guesses why the state is making this move now?" I asked each provider. "This just doesn't seem to make sense."

JT, a counselor and advocate who wore cowboy boots and bolo ties, took no shit from anyone.

"The state has never wanted to pick up the tab for housing these teens on the streets. If they license teen shelters, they admit there are teens on the streets, and then they need to provide some sort of care and funding for the kids."

JT thought this could be a way to help the teens and create a steady funding source around the state for all kids to be helped off the streets. His logic made sense to me in the moment. Without a proper youth shelter license, Cocoon House was operating as a foster home with waivers to allow us to take in teens that weren't in foster care. We had a waiver for the number of kids we could take in: eight, instead of the usual maximum of six. We had a waiver for having one overnight staff person who traded their time for room and board, but wasn't really any of the kids' foster parent. We had a waiver to have one person overnight when the kids slept instead of two parents in our fake foster home.

We had a waiver to allow us to have volunteers on site, as long as they passed background checks. We had a waiver to allow us to take in babies with their moms. The list of waivers went on and on. A youth shelter license would acknowledge that these kids existed in our state, and they needed shelter.

I worked up the courage to call our local licensor, Mary. But if Mary knew anything about the youth shelter license, she was not revealing it.

"This is way above my pay grade. Go all the way to the top," she told me.

I met with the director of the region. Nancy said she'd look into it.

Weeks went by, and I wasn't getting any answers. I was chewing the inside of my left cheek, grinding my teeth in my sleep and waking up in a sweat. Something in my body was saying something wasn't right. I couldn't get any information from anyone.

Our County Children's Commission agreed to take on the issue and press for information.

The problems I had to think about: Would Cocoon House meet the new qualifications of a youth shelter license? What would be in the requirements? Our state was famous for writing up extensive requirements. Would I be able to give input into the license? Would we be able to get waivers? Could a youth shelter be sited in a residential house on a neighborhood street, or would it be expected to look like a facility rather than a house? What would be the building codes?

I was pacing back and forth while talking to people around the state. And asking anyone who I spoke with, "Why now? And why all the quiet secrets about it?"

A Children's Commission board member pried loose a draft of the license. He showed up at Cocoon House with a large manila envelope. I felt like I was being served a summons.

"Will you sit with me while I read it?" I asked, taking the envelope and pulling out a stack of pages listing the requirements for the youth shelter license.

"It's pretty bad," was all the commissioner said.

I nearly collapsed as I read while pacing in the small entryway of Cocoon.

"This will quadruple our operating expenses." I was stunned.

No volunteers could staff the site. We would need two full-time paid employees every single hour, day and night.

"Where will I get the money to do this?"

The Children's Commissioner shook his head. "I have no idea. But let's call a formal meeting with the state and bring the big Cocoon supporters to the table. We will start with negotiating for waivers to give you time to find this money."

It was an idea. I was all out of ideas as I read the pages of requirements. I called Cowboy Boots JT.

"The state is not looking at how to serve the kids. They are looking at how to shut the doors of the youth shelters. We need to do something."

We formed a statewide homeless-youth task force. Our goal was to get input into the licensing laws to ensure grassroots nonprofits could do the job the state was not willing to do.

The second goal of the task force was to have the state pay for the new expensive mandates.

We got nowhere on both counts. We weren't ready to do battle with the state. We were creating a task force out of a loose band of people around the state who were exhausted from trying to care for kids in their communities with very little money. We didn't have time to attend statewide meetings and become a task force. We had no experience advocating as one voice together. We had to learn how to do this. But first we had to meet each other, learn names, visit each other's programs, see what we could string together. It took time. Meanwhile, the state was moving ahead with its licensing laws. Our loose, newly formed task force was mowed over the way a skidder clears a forest.

The state would not offer a dime to cover costs in the youth shelter, but they did offer me a contract to help pay for some housing in the new building – 2 of the 16 new beds. Not much. I refused the contract. It wasn't that we didn't need the money. We needed every dollar offered. But the state wanted to decide who would get to stay in that housing. They also could pull kids out of that housing at any time.

We were making a promise to kids with the new building. The promise was they could grow up at Cocoon. As long as they followed the rules, no one would take away their housing. Cocoon House was in business because the state was ignoring these teens. I could not let the state have control over the beds.

The expensive licensing requirements passed the legislature as written. I didn't know what kind of licensing requirements we would face with the new building; we couldn't open it until we solved the sprinkler-system problem. But that would have to wait. Because right behind the youth shelter licensing requirements came the "Becca Bill."

Thank goodness we had formed the statewide task force because much more was at stake than the cost of running a shelter.

30

FIGHTING FOR TWO WORDS

We hide some of the most important things. I found part of the job of running a nonprofit was really being the finder of things: finding truth, finding kids, finding money, finding caring staff. I was always learning how to do the job I was doing. The problems that came toward me never gave me a chance to catch up.

It's impossible to know the things that are hidden from us. Sneaky things happened in the state legislature. I learned, tracking the Cocoon tax-savings bill that Jeri Costa sponsored, to read every single line in any bill moving through the legislature that concerned teens. Never just read some of it. Jeri taught me to read every version, as a bill changes day by day while moving from hand to hand – and again when it goes from the House to Senate. She explained that one representative might slip in a single word that changes everything and she didn't have time to read every word, so I needed to watch, read and advise her. The original bill might say that disaster supplies will be provided for everyone. The next day the word "not" could be added by a representative, and now the disaster bill you pushed for would say, "This bill does not provide disaster supplies for everyone."

I learned from the youth shelter license law that children who were homeless needed representation in the state legislature.

When an important food program for hungry children was being cut, a group of us from the homeless-youth task force swooped down on the state capitol, carrying forks and spoons and shouting "Pick on someone your own size!"

My daughters were attending rallies in the capital by the age of five, carrying painted signs about protecting food for every child. It embedded in them the necessity to stand up for others and with others.

I was a mommy, an executive director, and then I added to the list: an advocate in our state capitol.

After the youth shelter licensing went into effect, a new bill was circulating in our capitol – the Becca Bill.

Having an eye on our state legislature, I got an early draft to read. It called for courts to get involved in school truancy. In my training as a teacher, I never heard of such a thing. It read like a dystopian novel. Somewhere in the future, police would be involved in making sure teenagers were not truant from school.

At the very end of the draft of the Becca Bill, it mentioned "youth on the street." The bill required police to arrest any teens who were homeless or runaways and lock them in a detention facility.

If the Becca Bill passed, kids who were homeless would have a record, and they would be locked in a jail. Most kids in Cocoon House were not "runaways," they were "throw-aways." Our beds were filled with kids who were "left" on the street. They came home to an empty apartment when a parent left town without them. They were thrown out of their house because they were gay or using drugs. Some of their parents had serious problems of their own: addiction, schizophrenia, domestic violence, or they'd been arrested themselves. It wasn't just the kid's story; if we could find a parent, we spoke to them and confirmed what their child had said. These stories were so much a part of the adult world, kids couldn't make them up. There were details that you couldn't imagine, you could only know them if you lived them. And the kids we worked with had the scars from it.

Arresting kids wouldn't protect them, it would make the kids hide from police. Hiding deeper underground would leave kids more vulnerable to the pimps, drug dealers and gangs who dominated the streets.

It would take much longer for Cocoon House to reach a teen. The longer a teen was on the street, the worse things got for them.

I was frantic. What the hell had ignited the Becca Bill? Every bill comes from someone.

There is always a story and a person or group of people behind a bill. I had to find the story behind the Becca Bill. I searched newspapers around the state and learned that it was named for a young teen, Rebecca. The story was that Rebecca was murdered at age 13 after running away from home.

Thirteen. Murdered.

The anguish of a child murdered filled my chest. Grief, outrage and heartache were behind the Becca Bill. Tears rolled down my face. She was just a baby.

Why was she was running? It seemed like a crazy question, but I had too much experience with teens to let the story stop there. The bill was calling for the arrest of all teens on the street. I had to get involved. It was not a choice. I wanted to know more about why Becca ran away.

No one reported that.

I called representatives signing onto the bill. I asked if any of the representatives knew why Rebecca had run away. "No," they'd say. "And isn't that beside the point? Who knows why a 13-year-old does what they do?"

I needed someone who could dig deeper. I called my friend Bill, who worked in the prosecutor's office; he worked on behalf of children and how their cases were handled. When children were sexually assaulted, Bill cared about how they were interviewed and what the court process would be. He was like a patron saint of children in courtrooms.

The patron saint of children in courtrooms and I met for coffee. We were in a red upholstered booth in Carl's Bakery, a shop famous for its donuts and breakfast. Orders came through a small hole in the wall. The place was full of old-timers who were regulars – breakfast every morning, same time, same place.

Bill folded his hands on the table and said, "I am piecing together bits of things."

As reported in *The Seattle Times,* Becca's adoptive father said that when she was six months old, she was sexually abused in her natural parents' home. So, she came to live as a foster child with a family, and they eventually adopted her.

But the abuse didn't end there. When Becca was five, it was reported that she was again sexually abused, this time by an older adopted brother. The boy was sent to live elsewhere. They got help for Becca, but as she became a teenager, she was using drugs. Trauma, removal, assault – they all leave many scars.

Bill went on, "Her parents couldn't keep her from running. They may have thought that if only the police would have locked her up, she'd be alive."

What a heartache. I couldn't imagine the anguish these parents had gone through. They were trying to save their daughter. Of course they'd rather have some way to get her off the streets.

Bill and I went to Olympia, a two-hour drive each way to try to meet with representatives and talk about the harm the Becca Bill could do to kids who were homeless. Rebecca did deserve justice. Maybe wrongly, I told myself the murderer who found her could have grabbed her at any time. He could've grabbed her on the way to school. He could have grabbed her any place.

As we walked the halls of the state capitol, our hopes of convincing legislators diminished. Posters with blown-up photos of 13-year-old Rebecca were plastered on the walls everywhere. The campaign for the Becca Bill was galvanized by representatives and senators trying to do right by her grieving parents – and do right by Rebecca.

They had in their hands a bill that her parents wanted. How could you say no? Their child was murdered.

Each meeting Bill and I had with a representative went the same way. They looked at us, nodded, and responded with a version of, "There's a dead child's picture lining the halls. This bill is all we have."

They were right. Her parents deserved something. Becca deserved better.

There was no counter bill. There was nothing else to offer her parents.

However, locking kids up in cages was not good policy.

As the bill meandered through the capitol, it got stuffed with concerns from parents all around the state who couldn't get services for their kids, parents who were desperate to find help for their kids and were dealing with kids who were refusing to go to school, kids who had a variety of issues. The Becca Bill gained momentum as parents could see that the bill might provide help for them to get drug treatment for their kids, mental health assessments and counseling services.

The bill was offering hope and help to desperate families. I understood the need for some way to protect kids from harming themselves.

But the one sentence in the bill about locking kids in jail went against every piece of research and best practice for kids. The whole juvenile justice system was undergoing reform and realizing that engaging kids in programs and supports was far more effective than detention. But even the governor's juvenile justice task force couldn't convince anyone that the Becca Bill was moving away from best practices.

The patron saint of children in courtrooms and I returned to the state capitol. We shared research. All we could do was not give up.

Two of the biggest supporters of the bill were Norm Maleng, the King County Prosecutor, and a senator who had sponsored a bill to make any sex outside of marriage illegal, including any sex minors had. He was fine with locking up people of all ages for having sex. This is who I had to negotiate with: either the guy who wanted to arrest people for having sex or the King County Prosecutor. My odds were terrible.

I was invited to debate with Norm Maleng about the Becca Bill on a public radio show. I agreed to do it because it was the only way to discuss the Becca Bill with him. He would only do a radio show.

Norm Maleng was a seasoned lawyer and prosecutor. I was not a lawyer. I was never on a debate team in high school. I remember leaving social studies class in tears in high school when I was forced to debate a team of smart-ass boys.

Norm Maleng was a popular, tough prosecutor. I was nothing more than a fly in his soup. But Norm Maleng and I debated. I expected him to dominate the debate, but he didn't. He knew that locking kids up was not what the research was showing as helpful.

On the point of locking kids up, Norm Maleng and I agreed. There was nothing to debate about locking kids up. His experience and understanding of the research had him in agreement with me. I felt relieved and hopeless, because despite his understanding of the research, the line in the bill remained.

He was supporting the bill. He was dealing with the guy who murdered Becca. He understood the grief of Becca's parents. There is no pain like the pain of losing your child.

Like a gambler with bad luck, I was mush. The bill passed the House easily and was moving through the Senate. In the final days leading up to the vote on the bill, I had one thing left to try.

The crazy idea came to me in a dream.

The idea from my dream was to get two words inserted into the bill. The two words were: "or shelter."

Just before a vote on the bill, the sponsor of the bill, Senator no-sex-outside-of-marriage called me and said he was agreeing to insert my two words into the bill. Now, near the end of the Becca Bill, it read: A homeless youth will be taken to either a juvenile detention *or shelter*.

Now, the only question was, would those words stay in the bill through the floor vote?

While the senators voted, Representative Jeri Costa stood in the hall of the Senate. She had a phone off the hook so I could hear the vote at my desk hours away at Cocoon House in Everett. I listened as each person voted, gripping my pen, my desk, my stomach. The Becca Bill passed.

The words "or shelter" stayed in the bill.

Would the Becca Bill have saved Rebecca? I will never know the answer to this question. What her parents did while in enormous grief was write a bill to save *other* kids. At Cocoon House, we were trying to do the same thing. They had the bill named after their child. I had a shelter. Every moment I fought the bill, I knew we were on the same team.

It is in the places where we hurt that we are all connected.

31

SOMEONE IS LOOKING FOR ME

I remember walking to the mailbox. It was snowing. Soft, wet snow covered the driveway of my farmhouse. I walked out the kitchen door, following the circular driveway down to the road.

I collected a few envelopes, sifted through them as I walked back to the kitchen door. Junk mail. A party invitation. A postcard from a friend. A white envelope, handwritten address, return name I did not recognize, postmarked New Jersey. I knew only a few people in New Jersey from my college days. Who was this? I double checked – it was addressed to me.

I went in the kitchen, made some coffee. Sat down and opened the envelope.

Dear Sarri,
  You may not remember me . . .

He had been looking for me for years, this man who said he was my cousin. My cousin Mike.

How could this be?

I thought Mike and his siblings had died. I remembered his picture on the wall of the pink house. My three cousins, in small circular gold frames: Mike, Carol and Raymond. My mother had a sister – these were her children. They lived on the wall in the pink house. Their photos never got older. They were frozen in time at that age, on the wall.

When I was a little girl, they were part of my family. We played together. I adored my older cousin Mike. After I moved into my grandparents' pink house with my brother, I saw my cousins a few times and then, like my parents, they disappeared.

One day my aunt showed up at the pink house without my three cousins. She had two new children.

"Where are MY cousins?"

No one ever mentioned them. Their picture remained on the wall for all the years I grew up.

My three cousins, never mentioned again.

Once a year, on Thanksgiving, my brother and I went to my aunt's apartment in Brooklyn.

Adam knew only her new children as his cousins.

But when I went to her apartment in Brooklyn for Thanksgiving, I heard my older, disappeared ghost-cousins' voices in the hallway. I yelled out words in the empty hall and heard an echo come back. I was certain it was my cousin Mike in heaven. Inside the apartment, each Thanksgiving, I stealthily opened drawers and cabinets looking for signs of my cousins in my aunt's apartment. I found nothing. No toys, no games, none of their clothes, no pictures.

I thought they'd died in a car accident. I can't remember if I was told that they died or if I made that up.

My aunt had new children: a toddler and a new baby. Then a new husband. Her life went on with her new children, my new cousins.

Now, 30 years later, I was holding in my hands a letter from this person, a stranger, someone I no longer knew. My disappeared cousin. According to his letter, he had grown up in New Jersey. Only a few hours away from the pink house.

He grew up with his sister and brother; they lived with his father. His parents had divorced when we were young. His father got custody and moved them to New Jersey.

My head was swirling. I felt like I was tumbling down a mountain. Was I dreaming? I looked outside. I put on my jacket and went out into the snow. I breathed the cold air into my lungs.

Then I bent over and howled. My chest was pounding. I sat on the edge of my deck and cried as the snow covered everything. The grief of losing my cousin Mike, the grief I could never talk about as a child, came roaring through me. My grief was a wild bear. All the lies I was told as a child. All that was taken away. A grief I didn't have the words for.

My cousin's letter was several pages. He took time to tell me what happened to his sister and younger brother. He was returning to me a story of other missing children in my family.

He explained that his sister was well but wanted nothing to do with the family. I understood that – when Adam entered adulthood and took risks I couldn't stand to watch, we had to give each other a lot of space. As I was evolving, he was too. In time, he would find his better angels and build the family and home he hadn't had growing up. He healed many of the wounds in our family by walking through them directly and transforming his life. I understood my cousins must have had to make similar painful choices as they sought to heal.

Mike explained that his younger brother, my cousin Raymond, was no longer alive. When he turned 18, he was run over by a train.

Run over by a train.

Not every child could survive my family.

Raymond's real death was much worse than the death I'd imagined for him as a small child.

I was tangled in a live wire, getting electrocuted. It was another unbearable loss in my disfigured family tree.

My cousin Mike had been looking for me – for the lost parts of his family.

In the days, weeks and months ahead, broken bits of memories returned to me. Things that had been hidden, like old soft toys I had as a child. Memories of Mike, Carol and Raymond returned.

Mike was the leader of our little group. I followed on his heels. He made up stories. We pretended to be pirates, thieves, monkeys. Mike made shadow puppets on the wall with his hands; he whistled tunes for me to guess. We jumped rope and ran through alleyways in Brooklyn, playing hide-and-seek.

It was my first experience with the psychological phenomenon I had read about: suppressed memories. They flew around me like butterflies. I tried to catch each memory as it fluttered by, hoping it wouldn't disappear into the vastness again. These were my memories. Our childhood.

Why didn't my grandparents visit their grandchildren? Why didn't my grandparents take me to see my cousins? How did my family end up smashed to bits and hidden away from each other? I will never know the answer to this. I can't go back and change the story or change my grandparents.

My family was filled with terrible secrets and lies.

My grandmother insisted on telling me over and over that my mother was a very good mother and would have been a great mother if my father hadn't ruined her life. I never met that "good mother." Only once did my mother visit the pink house where I lived with my grandparents and stay overnight. Literally only once in 15 years, she stayed the night. And she set the house on fire with all of us in it.

My grandmother said she had fallen asleep with a lit cigarette and that caused the fire. My mother smoked her whole life, never once a fire anywhere. But she set the pink house on fire with all of us asleep.

I spent time with my mom throughout my teenage years. I drove a van for her illegally, before I had a driver's license, to take her to craft shows up and down the East Coast on weekends, while she sold lace clothing she made. I drove because my mother was high on heroin. We didn't eat meals until she was hungry. And then they weren't meals. My mother cooked nothing but spaghetti. Most of the time, I walked to the store and found something to eat.

She kept only cartons of wine by her empty refrigerator in a house my grandfather rented for her.

My mother was a talented artist, a clothing designer who made beautiful clothes. She sold them and then turned all her dollars into drugs. There wasn't a single day that my mother did the job of being a mom to me. My grandmother had imagined and invented a mother for me who never existed.

My grandfather insisted that my father was dangerous.

I got to know my father when I turned 18. He and I spent years repairing a broken bond. My father attended therapy with me to fix our relationship. He showed up every summer for three months to visit me in the Pacific Northwest. We had lunch out every Thursday in the summer together. I spent 25 years catching up with my father, taking trips with him, staying at his home, vacations, holidays, summers. I knew him very well.

My father was not dangerous. He was the guy who gave my daughter Aliza $40 to win a goldfish at the fair when she was seven years old. She turned the money into quarters and kept throwing quarters at the waterfilled bowls to win a goldfish. If the quarter landed in the bowl, she'd get the fish. He stood by laughing as she aimed 160 quarters at the bowls.

On a trip to Vancouver, Canada, I returned to our hotel to find my father on the balcony with my daughters, teaching them how to spit wads of paper through straws, aiming at pedestrians on the street below. My dad, who had ADD, was silly, reckless and impulsive. A big spender, he wasted money. He was generous, consistent and white-male privileged. He never missed a chance to have a conversation.

My grandfather did not want me to love my father. He made it seem like my father was the enemy.

I couldn't embrace my grandfather's lies and love my father and his parents. My grandfather couldn't tolerate me loving my father and being close to him, while my mother was incapable of being a mom.

My grandparents buried the truth like it was garbage.

I thought about how to write back to my cousin Mike. I wondered if he would be surprised that I became a family therapist. Would he be surprised that I was running a teen shelter for kids who had also come from very troubled families?

Because of the family I came from, I understood how some families could be confusing and full of problems. I became a family therapist to help people untangle the troubling things that happen inside of families.

There was so much hidden in my family.

My 18-year-old cousin, run over by a train. How could the life of my three cousins go unacknowledged? How could the death of Raymond never be mentioned? How was it we turned into half-children who were here but not here?

I thought about how much my cousin Mike had had to carry. I wondered how I could come from the sort of family where parents disappear, cousins are never spoken of, and one is run over by a train. I wrote back to my cousin Mike, letting him know how much he was missed by me and that I wanted a relationship.

I wanted to protect my twin daughters from everything inside my twisted family. I didn't share with them my family stories – they were simply not the sort of stories one tells a small child.

I thought of myself as a shield. I didn't want my daughters to inherit the legacy of my family.

In many ways, my daughters were not shielded. They were exposed to homelessness, a working mom, divorce, the shelter and to teens who had nothing. These were difficult truths. Not hidden.

I tried to protect Cocoon kids from pimps, murderers, laws to lock them up, violent families and trains.

But how do you stand in a place where the attacks are coming from inside your own family and be a shield?

I read my cousin's letter over and over, feeling smaller, younger and more vulnerable with every word. I had no shield.

32

OPENING DAY

Our license for the new building was suspended until I could pay for the missing sprinkler system. I had half the money because Rep. Jeri Costa had performed a miracle getting the bill signed in the capitol. I had no idea how to get the rest of the money.

Four years earlier, on the opening day of Cocoon House, a man known as The General had come to the shelter and given me his business card. I remembered him sitting in a chair across from me and handing me the card. He was older and struck me as someone deeply experienced. He had spent decades running the Medina Foundation. This was a family-run foundation using the proceeds from the century-old Weyerhaeuser Corporation. The foundation had deep roots in Washington. I had felt honored to meet The General. We'd talked for a few minutes. When he stood up to leave, he'd said, "If you ever run into trouble, you call that red phone number."

I saved this card in my wallet for four years. He seemed like a very important ally for Cocoon House. For years, I couldn't imagine what would make me call that number, but I knew it was good to keep.

I called him.

"Hi, you may not remember me. I run Cocoon House, and four years ago you gave me a card and said I could call you if I got in trouble. I'm in trouble."

He didn't ask what the problem was. He invited me to meet with him – immediately, in his office in downtown Seattle. I got in my car and drove 30 minutes to his office. It was a secure building. My door was opened for me in the parking garage by an attendant wearing a suit and tie, who escorted me into an elevator.

It seemed like I stepped into a palace. I got off the elevator and found myself in a room filled with magnificent art, a Dale Chihuly glass chandelier, yellow spires twisting out in all directions, and a Georgia O'Keefe painting with soft gray and touches of pink, Prussian blues and yellow streaks. I walked up to the O'Keefe painting. I had never stood so close to one of her paintings.

Not a single brushstroke visible.

A secretary welcomed me, and the garage escort left. After a few minutes of staring at the artwork, The General greeted me in his tailored suit and crisp white shirt. His shoes looked like they just came out of a box from Italy. I felt very poor. I was hoping that my shoes did not to leave a trail of dirt on the carpet as I followed him into his office with spotless glass tables and leather furniture.

The General sat behind a rectangular desk, polished and gleaming with the light from the sun pouring in. A full wall was glass, looking out over Puget Sound. I sat down on a black leather chair, wearing a blue dress that was too big and hung a bit from my shoulders. My dirty shoes didn't match my dress. I tearfully explained the sprinkler problem. I admitted I was a failure and shouldn't be running Cocoon House.

The General pulled a pad out of his desk and starting writing notes, probably about my failure.

He asked me to look up on the walls of his office and tell him what I saw. There were pictures of athletes on the walls, runners in running clothes, a skier on top of a slope, a gymnast poised ready to jump on a balance beam. All of them had famous familiar faces.

"I see world-class athletes."

"Yes. Each of those pictures is someone just before their Olympic event. Do you know why I wanted to collect the photos from the moment just before the event?"

"No." Tears streaked down my face, and I felt even smaller in the chair next to these world-class athletes. I felt like I was back in the courtroom – so small, I needed a phone book to sit on.

The General, in his well-fitting suit, said, "Sarri, it doesn't matter to me how they did in their race. What matters is they worked hard enough to get to that starting line. That is a true champion."

He continued, "It doesn't matter that you ran short for the sprinkler system. How many people do you think would go out and build Cocoon House?"

I shrugged.

He handed me a note from the pad he was writing on. It said, "You are a champion." Then he handed me a check for $40,000. No questions, no budget forms to give him. No grant application to fill out. He handed me what we needed. My search for sprinkler money was over. He was paying for the rest of the sprinkler system with $5,000 extra thrown in, just in case Cocoon needed it.

For the first time in a long time, I felt air rush into my body. I could exhale.

This was my second true lesson in leadership. My first lesson was "FIO": Figure it out. My second lesson was it didn't matter how you did in the race. It didn't matter if you had setbacks. What mattered was trying.

I left Seattle, dropped the check off with the staff at Cocoon and went home for a few days and cuddled up with my daughters. I felt this huge release, like a monster that had been holding me finally let go. Trauma relief.

When I returned to Cocoon House, I came in with a new attitude. I could not let others treat me like I had no abilities and no value. It wasn't just the kids I would need to advocate for. I would need to hold my ground more firmly. I allowed the county, the city and my board to sideline me during construction, thinking I was not "capable" of overseeing the project. But really, when it all went to hell, I was the one who had to come up with the solutions for the "experts."

I would need to go forward, not allowing others to dump problems on my desk. If someone was going to take responsibility for something, I would hold them accountable.

But I also understood that as director I was shouldering enormous responsibilities. I was being the responsible parent I didn't have growing up. And I was recreating my family. No one else was responsible. The weight of the nonprofit agency with an important promise to kids was always hanging over me. Every problem, big or small, stopped with me.

I had to learn how to share the problems.

All of us – the board, the staff and the kids – we all had to see ourselves as problem solvers.

I thought of building that capacity as a people-growing activity.

I spent a few days playing with my daughters. I hit the pause button on work. I was breathing deeper, sleeping better and laughing. My daughters were little giggling fountains. I could step into our little world, close the door behind us, take out our paints and draw animals, make up stories together and look for seashells on the beach.

When I felt recovered and rested, it was time to plan the ribbon-cutting ceremony for our new building.

I invited Rep. Jeri Costa to speak at the ceremony. She had done all the stunt work getting the bill passed to save us on taxes so I could pay for the sprinkler. It was a tough sell in our state capitol, because even though other communities could benefit from the bill, none had youth housing construction going on right then to benefit from the bill. Getting signatures on the bill was a debt that Jeri was incurring. She would owe favors back to every signer.

A few days before the ribbon-cutting, Jeri announced that the governor would be attending. He wanted to sign the "Cocoon" Bill at our building. The governor attending a ribbon-cutting at a building for our kids was a big deal. They announced it in the newspaper, and our community was excited.

On the night before the ribbon-cutting, I didn't sleep a single hour. I was just waiting for the first ferry boat to start up and drive over to the new Cocoon Complex. I was there to fuss over things being clean, help set up chairs, calm the nerves of staff and kids.

As I drove up to the building, I was shocked by what I saw on our brand-new building. I parked my car in our parking lot, then walked back to the north side of the building. It was visible to the street. A massive black swastika, 20 feet tall, had been spray-painted on the side of our brand-new building.

I am Jewish. This was intentional. The announcement was in the paper, and the governor would be here in six hours. The swastika would take all the attention from opening the new building. I sat on the sidewalk and hung my head, tears streaming down my face. I called Danny. I told him we had a giant swastika on the building. I didn't know what else to say. He said he was on his way.

My next call was to the police chief. I had his private phone.

"Chief, we have a swastika on our building."

He said, "I'll be right over."

In my four years of operating Cocoon House, the chief and I had several meetings and phone calls. All meetings were at his office. He had never met me at the building. I was grateful he was on his way. I wasn't sure I could stand up. I sat by the swastika.

The chief arrived in 15 minutes.

I confessed to him I felt done.

"I don't want to do this job anymore. I am sick of fighting for everything." I stood in front of the swastika. Chief stood on my side.

He listened. I went over every struggle I had endured to make this organization work, ending with, "I don't have this in me. Not a swastika.

"I don't even want to stay in Washington after seeing this."

I grew up in a community that was mostly Jewish. I had a neighbor at the end of my block who had a number tattooed on her arm by the Germans. I was born 15 years after the Holocaust. It was raw and smoldering in the minds of every person in my neighborhood growing up.

The repulsion of the swastika shot through me. I bent forward and vomited on the sidewalk. Chief held my shoulders. He offered me a tissue and gum. He listened to me until I had no words, just bile.

He waited until I had nothing else to say.

"You can't let them win. This is not when you quit. It's a mean, ugly thing. This ugly spray job was done in the middle of the night by a guy too scared to show his face. This was done by a chickenshit.

"This was not someone brave, not someone like you. You can't let this chickenshit scare you away. I'm going to have armed plainclothes police all over this place. This chickenshit just wants attention." He continued, "Don't give him that. My cops will set up a post."

He went to his squad car to make some calls. Just then Danny arrived. He was walking toward me with a paint can, a roller brush with a long handle, a paint tray and a big smile on his face.

"Nothing a little paint can't fix," he said.

When he opened the paint can, the paint fumes jolted me. The smell of fresh paint was faintly lingering all around our new building. We had a new building. We had a ribbon to cut. Kids who were excited about their home and had not seen the swastika on their new home.

They would not see the swastika.

I needed to get up and put a smile on. Focus on the good. See the good.

But the pain ran deep.

33

456

The new building was made possible by generous support, and I had some people to thank. I pulled up early in the morning, 5am, to meet at a warehouse filled with drivers of the brown UPS trucks before they started their route. Everyone was wearing brown shirts and brown shorts. I looked in the group for my local neighborhood driver.

I was there to thank them for their work and the company's gift to Cocoon House. UPS had helped me build a commercial kitchen for our new motel.

Our motel no longer looked like a motel. It was now housing for 16 teenagers. The parking lot was torn out, and we planted grass. We built a kitchen lodge to enclose the grassy courtyard.

The lodge was a living room, dining hall and hang-out space for the teens, and it had a commercial kitchen. The commercial kitchen was a leap for a youth housing program. I was taking a gamble, and UPS was investing in the risk I was taking.

I came to thank them for a $50,000 gift for the kitchen, but also for being willing to try a concept that was new. UPS had a long history supporting children and teens through their foundation, the Annie E. Casey Foundation. Annie E. Casey had lived in Seattle and struggled to raise her four kids on her own. Her eldest son Jim started a messenger service in 1907 to help her support the family. That messenger service became United Parcel Service. In 1948, the Annie E. Casey Foundation supported children and teens who were facing many challenges. This foundation understood how to make a difference in the lives of kids who were on their own.

They understood my concept and thought it was worth a shot. The kids that would live at Cocoon Complex – Tray, Lilly, baby Will and the other kids – would be with us for one or two years. This was not a shelter. This was long-term housing. Of course, they would need to eat, and none of the renovated rooms had a kitchen in them. I wasn't concerned about teaching the kids the basics of cooking. That was easy.

But how would they get jobs and be able to support themselves after they left Cocoon Complex? That's where the commercial kitchen came in.

Of course, the trades and completing their educations was one path to self-sufficiency. But as we got to know the kids who had been homeless, we came to realize how many had very disrupted educations. They had been in multiple schools.

Researchers have found that every time a kid leaves a school, they fall behind six months. Some of our kids had been in five or six school districts. A few were still trying to attend high school when they came to us, but that was not the norm. We would reconnect them to school when possible. We even opened a school at the motel in partnership with the Everett School District. We knocked out four precious walls of housing space to make a classroom.

But I just couldn't bet that school or the trades were going to hook every kid into a future.

How would they become self-supporting adults – how could they not return to homelessness?

As I walked the streets of Everett wondering about this, I noticed the town had a lot of restaurants. How many restaurants were there? I did a little research and found there were 456 licensed restaurants.

My big gamble was to build a commercial kitchen inside of the complex. A full-scale restaurant-size kitchen with restaurant-size ovens, a dishwasher, walk-in fridge and freezer. My hope was that the Cocoon kids would learn to use the equipment and have a bit of an advantage over any other teen applying for a restaurant job.

There were so many skills our kids needed to learn to become self-sufficient in a short time. I was betting that the commercial kitchen would give our kids one more boost. When our stainless-steel commercial appliances were installed, the shiny, oversized equipment was intimidating. The stove looked dangerous. The walk-in fridge – what if a kid got locked in there? The mixer looked like it could take off fingers. What was I thinking?

My staff team – Tempel, Kim and Danny – did not know how to work anything in the kitchen. My loyal staff looked at me, bewildered.

Tempel, trying to be helpful, asked, "Do you have any manuals?"

He was willing to figure it out. I loved that about him. I knew he would do it too. I thought of missing fingers and burned faces. I looked at my loyal, willing-to-do-anything team and realized this was too much to ask of them. I put out an ad in the *Herald* to hire a cook.

I did not pitch the concept to our funders as, "We don't know how to turn on anything in the new kitchen and we're scared to be locked in the fridge." I sold it to funders as a nutrition program. We were going to create a healthy nutrition program, and we needed a chef to help us.

The funders loved that idea.

The tricky part was not finding a chef who could work commercial appliances, but a chef who would have 16 teenage sous-chef apprentices, all of whom had been homeless and weren't always great rule followers.

Sabina answered my ad and came on a motorcycle wearing a fringed black leather jacket. She was the boss of that kitchen from the moment she walked in the door. She had a good measure of tough that I would trust in a kitchen filled with dangerous equipment. She made every kid get a health department card to join her in the kitchen. She taught every kid how to cook. If you wanted to eat, you had to learn.

She also kept her eye on me. Sabina noticed when I was exhausted, always searching for the money we needed. She'd send a kid in with a hot plate of food. The kid, beaming, would say, "Look what Sabina and I made. I just want you to taste it." The food was delicious. When kids graduated from Cocoon, Sabina made each kid a recipe book with their favorite foods.

Sabina sometimes came with her mother. Momma showed up with her apron and made dishes from recipes passed down in her

Latinx family. Momma had stories about everything she cooked. She taught the kids that food was love, and love was passed down to us through food.

The kids lit up when Momma was on campus.

As I thanked the UPS drivers for our kitchen, one guy in brown shorts asked, "Did the commercial kitchen work? Did the kids get jobs?"

"Now the restaurants come to us, posting their help-wanted ads on our bulletin board inside Cocoon Complex," I told him. "Our kids have found more than jobs – they've found a way into the community."

I also told them about Sabina and the kids taking catering orders for nonprofit meetings.

"I had just hoped our kids would learn employable skills," I said. "But what I hadn't thought about was the deeper thing that happened. The kids, who were homeless and seen as worthless, are now seen as having value."

A job for our kids was much more than a job. Synergy was the magic of social activism. Things added up. The whole was more than the sum of the parts. Unexpected benefits happened all the time. It was the dopamine of nonprofit work: tipping points and surprising ripple effects.

34

TRAY, PART II

On his third attempt, Tray passed his GED.

Tempel cried. Tray cried. We all cried. It didn't seem possible. The battle was over: Tray had his GED. He passed the math section.

It was such a big moment. I thought, "This kid deserves an Olympic medal."

Two other Cocoon kids also had big achievements around the same time. Ellie got a full-time job and was moving into an apartment. Ellie had spent much of her young teen years in detention. But now she had relinquished her old crowd of friends and was no longer a follower.

She had dreams and goals and wanted "a clean life."

Roxy was also ready to move on from us. She'd finished high school and was ready to start community college.

Why not an Olympic medal for each of them?

I ordered the biggest medals I could find.

Our staff gathered up chairs in our new kitchen-lodge at Cocoon Complex, a room four times the size of the shelter's living room. Oh, the pride we felt as the lodge was decorated with paper streamers. Poster-board signs drawn with markers by the other kids and staff to congratulate the kids getting medals. "You are a butterfly!"

We lined up the metal chairs in two groups, like seating for weddings. The room filled with staff and teens and board members and a few community members. We ran out of chairs. A few people stood in the kitchen's bathroom door, peeking out to watch. Our three honored Cocoon kids walked down the middle aisle between the chairs. Tray had on his church shirt and tie, suit pants and shiny brown shoes. Ellie was in a dress, sandals with heels and makeup; her hair was styled and pinned up. Roxy was also in a shirt and tie, black high-top sneakers and black pants.

The three of them were glowing. Tray was sweating a little around his forehead, nervous, but looked at the crowd and smiled.

Leaning against the back wall, I felt the pride and recognition aimed at our three kids. Kids who are on their own rarely ever receive recognition. I wondered how many awards each of these kids had in their lives. How many thresholds had they crossed alone? How many times were the medals, the balloons, the signs for them? Did they know what it felt like when someone was cheering for them? Did they know what it sounded like when a whole room stood up and clapped for them?

I didn't know at that moment that we were starting a ritual. The Butterfly Ceremony would hold for decades. A ritual, a rite of passage, for kids to pass from adolescence to young adulthood, from high school to trade school, from adolescence to military service, from addiction to sobriety, from the past to the future, from disconnection to community, from isolation to belonging.

It would be more than the balloons, more than a white sheet cake where they smeared their names, more than the round medals on red-white-and-blue ribbons around their necks. It was the hopes and dreams of the staff who had supported them each step of the way. They needed to cross this threshold with the kids they cared for. They needed to see kids succeed. When they looked at kids who had suffered so much, they needed to know better things were possible. The Butterfly Ceremony was their moment too.

A few members of our Cocoon community were present at that first Butterfly ceremony, board members and volunteers. They too could see that Cocoon House was doing what we all hoped it could do.

Tray had his GED, he had his medal. There was cake and cookies and a room filled with laughter and music. They passed an envelope around to collect money for Tray's plane tickets.

I stepped outside and watched through the glass windows. People were congratulating Tray for his GED. I was thinking about how much more he had achieved in life than that.

Our final goal was to get his sisters. He'd waited two years.

I reached out again to the state of Mississippi. Tray was turning 18. He would lose his housing soon. Our license didn't allow us to keep him beyond his 18th birthday.

At last, Mississippi agreed to let his sisters go to Grandma's. Mississippi may have been waiting until he was of legal age, so if something happened to Grandma, there would be a next of kin to be the guardian for his sisters.

The great-big-hearted kid we all loved and cherished, the kid who was loyal and responsible, was going home. He wore a suit on the day he met with his sisters to tell them they were all going home to Grandma's. I don't know if those little ones remembered Grandma, but Tray remembered for them. He took the girls by the hand, and with his strong boundaries and values that could not be broken, boarded a plane to Grandma's house.

We said goodbye to the most thoughtful soul I had ever known. His patience was a spiritual lesson. He waited for his sisters, even though it meant his life was on hold, even though he had to live in a shelter, even though he was just a kid. Even though he was powerless over the decision-makers. Even though all he had experienced was abandonment. He would not abandon his sisters. Tray had faith. He believed in God.

When I started out at Cocoon House, religious people called me asking if they could take the kids to church on Sunday. At first it put me off. I had no experience of church. I didn't want to force religion on the kids. I didn't want them forced into beliefs they didn't have or want.

But eventually I decided I had been wrong about church. Time and time again, I learned from the kids how much comfort they found when they found God. The idea of a loving God gave them something their families couldn't. I learned from the kids that a spiritual home was a home. Finding God, restoring faith, belonging to a community, having a spiritual home was a saving grace for some of our Cocoon kids.

Though I don't subscribe to any of the religions our Cocoon kids found, I am a believer that having a spiritual home helps with the tougher things in life. It's difficult to explain to nonbelievers. I understand the skepticism. I had plenty of it myself. But for some kids, it offered something they needed. It was good for them. It nourished them. It healed them.

Tray had more capacity inside to carry his burdens than anyone I knew. It may have been because he had a deep spiritual connection to God.

35

LILLY TRYING

Lilly and Will moved into our new building. Will had a crib in Lilly's room. Lilly's room was like an overstuffed junk drawer – anything could be found in there. Piles of clothes covered every bit of furniture. No matter how many times Kim went in and organized the room with her, sorted dirty from clean and bagged up trash, Kim would always find things that were concerning. One time she found a handful of staples and thumb tacks in Will's crib.

Lilly was a tough kid who was often fighting with staff. She could be oppositional, belligerent and stubborn. Around me, she would calm down and act more respectful. But overall, she was resistant to rules, the staff and the demands of parenting.

Lilly attended school and was frequently given detention for arguing with her teachers. We required her to attend a teen parenting program two nights a week. In the parenting program, she learned about stages that babies go through and how to meet her son's needs. She was mentored daily in parenting skills at Cocoon and her high school. She spent time each day in the daycare center with a teacher who worked with her and Will and the other babies.

The progress was not visible.

I had to make calls to Child Protective Services. They didn't remove Will because we had so many staff with eyes on him that, in theory, he was safe. We continued to make mandated reports.

Lilly and I would sit together and talk about why Child Protective Services was being called this week. I hoped there was some benefit in these conversations. But I can't say I saw her behavior change.

She wasn't able to manage the responsibility. She didn't want to hurt Will; she just couldn't grasp how vulnerable he was.

All the staff got frustrated with Lilly. I heard shouting when Lilly trudged across the outdoor courtyard in her pajamas, in the rain and cold, with Will wearing only a diaper.

"It is only for a minute!" Lilly would shout.

"It is freezing outside!" Sabina wouldn't tolerate this.

"No breakfast. Leave the baby with me and march right back upstairs and get clothes and a blanket for this baby."

"Fuck you!" Lilly walked off.

Most of the time staff members were patient, but there were moments when Lilly pushed everyone's buttons.

As Will approached his first birthday, and after eight months of parenting classes, Lilly came to me and closed my office door. She wasn't angry, she wasn't coming in after a storm with a staff member. She was calm, not yelling.

She sat on the edge of my desk.

"I want to put Will up for adoption."

I listened. Looking at her brown eyes and soft round face, I wondered if she was just having a terrible day. Maybe she was depressed.

"Why do you want to him up for adoption?"

She stated without emotion, "I'm not ready to be a parent. I'm not good at this. I'm not getting good at this."

She had been listening. What she learned in parenting class was not what we what planned. We'd hoped she would learn skills and feel more able to parent. But what she learned was that she didn't have what it takes to be a parent. Not yet. She learned that she wasn't ready.

"I want Will to have a real mom and dad. I want him to have two parents who are already grown up."

Lilly went on, "I can only handle this because I have Kim and Sabina and all the other staff helping me. I could never do this on my own. I want Will to have a home, not a teen housing program. I want Will to have his own bedroom. I want him to have brothers and sisters. I want him to go to nursery school, not a high school for teen moms."

She wanted Will to have what she could not give him – and what she couldn't have for herself.

In that moment, I saw Lilly as the responsible mom we wanted her to become. She was seeing things from Will's perspective. She wanted her child to have more. Every mom wants this.

Lilly wasn't a grown-up. Parenting classes could not make her older or more mature. But she was growing up. This was the first time I heard Lilly talk about the future, both hers and Will's.

She was standing in Will's tiny baby shoes. She was having empathy for Will.

Will was always riding on her hip, missing his naps. She never left him in his crib or crying. I wondered what separating would be like for Will and Lilly. I didn't think, when it came down to it, Lilly could separate from Will.

Not once did any of the staff at Cocoon ever think of adoption as an option for Will. Will and Lilly were bonded.

I called a meeting with Kim, Lilly and Lilly's teen-parent coach, Marika. Marika had long, jet-black hair. She was tall. I looked up to meet her eyes. She wore a wrap dress and boots, and a thick gold chain hung from her neck. She carried a large purse that was more like a weekend-away bag. Marika set her bag down. I introduced myself and shook her hand. Kim introduced herself, reminding Marika of who she was, though it wasn't necessary. Kim had attended several parenting classes with Lilly.

I asked Lilly to explain to Kim and Marika what she wanted for Will. I knew she would need tremendous support to go through an adoption process.

Kim, our staff person, had been adopted. Kim's brow furrowed. She did this when she was thinking. Kim asked Lilly if she was sure about this. "Would you be interested in an open adoption?" Kim was always ready to lay the bricks on the road for whatever lay ahead. I loved that about Kim. If we have an idea, let's make the path.

The teen-parent coach, Marika, had been a teen parent. The idea of Lilly putting Will up for adoption sent her spiraling. She lost it. She jumped out of her chair and pointed her finger at Kim and me and yelled that this was our idea, not Lilly's. She was stamping her boots and cursing at us.

I wasn't expecting this. It was very normal to have a teenager pop off. But the teen-parent coach was expected to hold it together.

I had to switch gears and try to de-escalate the coach. I asked Lilly to take a break from the meeting. I promised we'd get back to her. Lilly didn't need to see Marika out of control, though it was too late – there was no unseeing what had just happened. I walked Lilly out of my office and said, "I'll take care of this."

I returned to my seat and thought about the three of us.

The three staff surrounding Lilly had all been in her story in some way. I was removed from my parents. Kim was adopted. Marika had been a teen mom. I wondered if we could navigate this without our own stories.

Rather than confront Marika on her unprofessional behavior, I met her where she was.

Lilly was a kid. She had tried to learn how to parent. She didn't believe she was ready to parent. As Will grew, Lilly could see his needs were changing and Lilly didn't know how to meet his continuously transforming needs. Most teenagers are not ready to be parents.

"Marika, what you could do as a young teen is remarkable. You raised your son. Not every teen can do this. This was not my agenda for Lilly either. I can't imagine the heartache of her separating from her son. But Lilly said what none of us could. She can't do it.

"This is the first time I have heard Lilly thinking about the future. You helped her be able to do that. This is the first time I heard Lilly think of all the things she wanted for Will. You helped her do that. You helped. This wasn't the outcome you expected. None of us did."

I worked for the next hour to help Marika return to a state of calm and trust. Her own trauma had been triggered. She sat in her seat, crying.

"Marika, did someone try to take your baby from you when you were a teen?"

She nodded, then shook her head, holding a tissue in front of her mouth. She waved her hand. She couldn't speak.

"I get it, Marika." Kim and I sat with her. Her eyes were closed. She was reliving something that happened a long time ago. It didn't matter. What mattered was that we were staying with her.

Marika opened her eyes. She wadded up the tissues into her purse. Kim asked if she wanted some tea.

"I'm okay. I get it. Can you please wait? Don't rush her. Lilly may change her mind."

I reassured Marika there was no rush. But Marika didn't know Lilly the way we did. Lilly's mind was made up.

Marika was in her own secondary trauma. I was growing a space in my heart to see this. I couldn't demand Marika be any other way. I felt her pain. I saw her wound. I wanted to make this better for her, but I couldn't. Neither could Lilly.

Lilly had her own path.

36

THANKSGIVING

There was some confusion for my daughters about my work. Mrs. Haugen, a warm, engaging first-grade teacher, asked her class how they would spend Thanksgiving.

"What will your family be doing for Thanksgiving?" I imagined the eager six- and seven-year-olds raised their hands, stretching their rib cages to be picked. I had seen this many times when I volunteered on Fridays, eager little hands waving in the air.

Aliza explained that she would visit Mommy's other houses. "My mommy has a hundred kids, and they live in two houses across the ferry."

Mrs. Haugen struggled to make sense of this. Aliza was an honest kid, not prone to telling lies in first grade.

"Who were all these other kids? Are these brothers and sisters?" Mrs. Haugen was trying to fit this into some sort of family.

"No, they're mommy's other kids in her other houses."

Mrs. Haugen could not make sense of Aliza's story and she cared enough to phone me. Mrs. Haugen, tired from a day of first graders' boisterous energy, got right to the point.

"I know this call seems out of the blue, but how many kids do you have? I thought it was just the twins?"

"It is just the twins."

"Aliza thinks you have two other houses filled with, and I am quoting here, 'a hundred other kids.' What is she talking about?"

"Oh, that. Yes, I can explain."

I tried to imagine how the shelter and renovated motel looked in the eyes of my daughters.

The rooms filled with adolescent boys and girls with hair dyed black, green, red and purple; with piercings; with holes in their jeans. Teens sleeping in bunk beds. The twins had only known this scene from the time they could walk. How else could it be explained?

As usual, we would spend Thanksgiving with the kids in mommy's other houses.

Thanksgiving preparations started a few days beforehand. Community members, strangers, drove up to Cocoon House, popped their trunks and carried bags of groceries to the door. We got more food than anyone could eat in one Thanksgiving meal. Our freezer was full of turkeys. Our fridge was full of side dishes, mashed potatoes, macaroni salad, hazelnut salad, broccoli salad and coleslaw. Every counter space in the kitchen had a pie on it – apple pies and pumpkin pies. We filled the laundry room with jugs of cider, cases of Coke.

I diverted the cars to stop the incoming food. I sat on the steps of the shelter as car after car pulled up. "We really can't accept any more food. We have plenty. Thank you. Bless you. Yes, all the kids will have Thanksgiving dinner. Please take your food to the food bank."

Thanksgiving day, I got to the shelter house at 8:30am, early. Taneesha met me at the door. She was 17, Black, and seemed more mature than most teens her age. She and her 3-year-old son were staying at Cocoon House.

"Good morning! Happy Thanksgiving! Come see the kitchen." Taneesha was already dressed in jeans and a white T-shirt. An apron was over the top. She had a pair of scissors in her hand.

"I'm just stringing the turkey."

I followed her, tiptoeing on the wooden floors, trying not to wake the other kids. No other teens were in the living room. Taneesha's son was on the brown couch asleep in pajamas, blankets whirled around him.

She was cleaning off a turkey in the sink. Singing.

"Taneesha," I whispered, "You don't have to cook. I got this." I gave her a hug.

"Have you seen all this food? I've never seen so much food! I am cooking this morning." There was no stopping Taneesha. Her eyes twinkled. She swayed and hummed.

Skye was at the desk by the front door in skates. He high-fived my daughters, who had followed me into the shelter. They were no longer behind me, but standing side by side at the desk with Skye. He asked what they were going to cook. My girls told him at the same time they were going to the complex and see what Sabina was cooking. But they were eager to show Skye what they made. They scrambled out the front door to the car and carried in Pyrex pans of sweet potatoes and a bag of marshmallows. They carried their goods into the kitchen.

"Oh, I'll take those!" Taneesha flashed a big smile to Somer and Aliza. They handed her their offering.

Things looked calm at the shelter. Skye called out in a loud whisper, "Hey, ask Taneesha if you can see her deviled eggs."

Taneesha poked her head out of the kitchen, "Did someone say deviled eggs? Yes, I heard that!" She brought a bowl out that could only be lifted with two hands.

"How many eggs have you made?" I stared into the metal bowl.

"I think that was 75."

Taneesha was so happy I didn't want to dampen her enthusiasm, so I said to myself, "We'll never eat all these eggs."

"I'll try those eggs." I reached out for one, thinking, "Someone needs to eat them."

Somer and Aliza looked into the bowl and backed away.

"I don't think they are hungry, Taneesha."

Taneesha shrugged and popped a deviled egg into her mouth and then returned the bowl to the fridge. She was glowing. Her electricity charged the whole house.

"Thank you, Taneesha. We are heading over to the complex. I promised the girls they could help Sabina this morning."

We walked around the block to the complex.

It was quiet. The teens were still sleeping, all 16 of them. I smelled coffee and cinnamon. Sabina held out two aprons for my daughters.

"You are just in time." The aprons were sized for a teenager and draped to my daughters' ankles. They followed Sabina like little ducklings.

"Time to make more cinnamon buns," she said. Much better than turkey. The girls knew they could count on Sabina.

I poured a cup of coffee and warmed my hands. My daughters were behind the kitchen partition with Sabina.

Karla pulled into the parking lot. Even on Thanksgiving morning, she wore a skirt and blouse. She pulled a raincoat on and belted it as she walked in the door. I was in jeans and a sweater I had knitted. I welcomed her in.

"I can only stay for a few minutes," she said. "I have some news." She took a deep breath as I poured her coffee. We sat at a long wooden table in pink foam chairs.

Sipping from her thick white coffee mug, she explained that the nonprofit organization where she worked was being merged with two other nonprofits, and her Teen Advocates program was being eliminated. She wanted it transferred to Cocoon House.

Karla and I were whispering. I didn't want anyone to overhear that I was dealing with agency business on Thanksgiving. I bowed my head closer to Karla as we talked.

Karla would be taking on a much bigger leadership role, but she wanted to protect the Teen Advocates program.

"Please, take them." She had tears in her eyes. She pulled a tissue from the pocket of her raincoat. "I know you will look after them and keep the program just as it is." I pulled Karla into my arms, her raincoat swishing against my gray sweater.

"Don't worry. We'll figure it out."

Karla left. I felt the weight of her sorrow and tried to bury it deep inside.

I returned to my daughters kneeling on stools at the metal island, while Sabina instructed them on how to swirl cream over the top of the hot, curled cinnamon buns.

I added more coffee to my mug. I had no space to take on more. Like the overstuffed freezer and fridge overflowing with food, there was no place in my life to put more.

A poem from Somer drifted into my mind. It was called "If My Mommy Had a Hundred Hands." That said it all.

Yet the Teen Advocates had to be rolled into Cocoon somehow – the kids needed the advocacy. I looked out the sliding doors to the cream-colored two-story building. Every purple door had two kids to a room. I wondered where I would put the Teen Advocates.

I wasn't trying to grow Cocoon House. People kept dropping things off at the doorstep: more kids, a new building and now the Teen Advocates.

Saying yes to the Teen Advocates meant so many things.

Yes, they would still work out of their cars; yes, they would still help thousands of kids get whatever they needed; yes, they would have money to buy essential items for kids.

But they would have to move from their home office to a new one. They would need a new home. The Teen Advocates were being adopted by Cocoon; would the staff want to be adopted?

How did the Teen Advocates know they could trust me? After losing their home agency, they would wonder how stable Cocoon was. Would their jobs last? Would I change their jobs?

All the words for the experience were triggering: "blending" staff teams, "adopting" the program, "moving." I would need to be patient and support five staff people through the transition.

It couldn't be helped. They were human. The thing we wanted them to bring to the job – their care and empathy and support for the kids – was also what made them vulnerable too.

I had no more time to think about it. It was Thanksgiving. Our kids were waking up, we would play games, cook, eat, go to a movie.

I returned to the joy of the day: the time together with the big Cocoon family. The kids were each carrying difficult memories and loss from their own families. There were lots of feelings. I was amazed at how well they were coping. The kids were excited, bubbling, laughing.

But I knew that it could be full of memories, and many would miss their families.

What we offered was not "culturally competent" for everyone. We were a diverse group from many backgrounds – staff and kids. It would have to do. With staff and kids from all different backgrounds, what I offered was probably inadequate. I did not really grasp racism back then. I had always worked with kids of different races. And yet, in the 1990s we didn't talk about race. I am certain I missed cues due to my own racial blindness.

Only two decades later am I learning about racism and beginning to see the tentacles of living in a white supremacist culture back then. I know I must have missed some of the important ways to honor each child's culture too. I knew there was always so much missing for the kids on a holiday. For the kids at Cocoon, just below the surface, there was always a layer of intense grief.

I was afraid to admit to myself how difficult it was to hold such a large space filled with so many emotions. I had my eyes on everyone, a lookout, making sure each kid was okay enough and not suicidal through the holiday.

But this Thanksgiving, the kids seemed ready to celebrate.

37

JOHN DOE

Cocoon House was a vulnerable place. We were part of the community, and lots of people dropped by to meet with me. No appointments needed; it was just normal for people to visit and ask to speak with me. Sometimes I was at Cocoon, sometimes I was home with my daughters.

People were always coming and going with donations for the shelter and the complex, too. We didn't have bulletproof glass or an alarm system. We didn't have cameras watching the doors. We did not feel unsafe.

Even after the person put the swastika on the building, I didn't feel unsafe. I just felt heartbroken.

I was never afraid of a teen we served. The kids who came to us were not looking for a fight; they were looking for shelter and safety.

A few times a drunken angry parent showed up at our door in the middle of the night wanting to see their kid, but it was rare. We would have to call the police to assure they got home safely, and then we'd set up a meeting with their teen and a counselor to help, in daylight.

Then one day I walked into the complex, and Kim met me with her brow furrowed. She took me by the elbow, both of us stopping on the cement walkway inside the courtyard. "A crazy man showed up. He wanted to see you. He had a gun, and he threw a stack of these copies of a paper into the air calling for the closure of Cocoon House. And then he left."

She stopped talking. Her gaze was searching.

"Who is this? He had a gun?" I wondered if I had heard her right.

"He was yelling he wanted to see you. We told him you weren't here. Sarri, please don't meet with him, he is crazy."

Kim was protective. She, like the rest of the staff, was always watching out for me. Like they knew I was missing some of my protective instincts.

I didn't have any idea who the person was. I know now, but I'll call him John Doe.

A few days later, I got a call from United Way, one of our funders. The director told me a man had visited them and told them I gave his daughter an abortion in the bathroom of Cocoon House.

"Can you tell me what he looked like? I don't do abortions and I did not give his daughter an abortion in our bathroom. Did he give you the name of his daughter?"

It was the same guy with the gun. Over the next two weeks, I got calls from every major grantor to Cocoon House. Our funding sources were public record, so he had no trouble finding who to go see. I even got a call from the governor's office.

Then John Doe returned to Cocoon Complex, terrorizing the staff with more pictures of guns.

He said, "These are for Sarri."

I didn't know what the gun photos meant, but I interpreted them as a threat. I called the police chief. He posted plainclothes police around Cocoon House. He also had plainclothes police where I was guest speaking. A police officer who was a friend of mine offered me a bulletproof vest to wear outside of Cocoon. I kept it hidden in the trunk of my car. I didn't want my daughters to find it.

Geoff, a Cocoon board member and attorney, wrote a letter explaining to every funder that this had been investigated at Cocoon House. What we had learned was one of the Teen Advocates had given his daughter food. The advocates could get kids school supplies, clothing, food, counseling and emergency support.

One of our teen advocates had given food to a girl who was asking for food.

Seemed reasonable.

The parent was angry about this and knew he couldn't get anyone to hear him on giving food to a kid, so he made up this crazy story and told it to every funder and every official he could find.

Each official met with him and listened to his story. At one point, a well-intentioned funder thought I should help this guy calm down by having a sit-down meeting with him.

Tank Girl went berserk. "We don't negotiate with terrorists!" She was doing circles around me with her armored truck.

I refused to meet with John Doe. That was a firm no. He had showed up with guns. He had issued warnings. From a clinical psychological perspective, I knew it was important to believe people when they give you warnings.

I had two daughters at home. I was not about to get shot in the head because someone felt entitled to threaten their mom and tell lies everywhere and try to shut Cocoon House down.

I told the County Executive, United Way and the Governor that it was not my job to put myself in harm's way to make anyone feel better.

Board members, funders and elected officials asked what I was going to do about him.

I did nothing. I would not put any energy into him. I had more than enough valuable things to do. There was no point in me meeting him. I would not shut down the Teen Advocates. I would not close Cocoon House. He was why we existed. How could I explain that to him? When Tim came by the complex, checking for repairs there and at the shelter, I mentioned John Doe. Tim dropped his usual smile, pulled out a small notepad and wrote notes while thinking out loud.

"We will put in a locking gate at the complex. Cameras for each of the doors. Both buildings. I'll get some volunteers to wire the windows with an alarm."

John Doe was another trauma trigger for me. His delusions, how far he was willing to go and the lies he told – it all reminded me of my family.

He was like my grandfather, with the storms in his head. I had no way to stop this guy. I could just ignore him on the outside. But inside, I knew he was there.

Yet in some respects I was numb to him. There was something not right about how calm and unmoved I was. Losing my ability to feel the fear and anxiety may have looked to some like professionalism. To me, it was a sign of secondary trauma: not feeling. I could feel some things, but for John Doe, I felt nothing at all.

I noticed Kim's alarm, my board's concern and Tim showing up battening down the buildings, adding locks, fencing, surveillance and alarms. I of course wanted that protection for the kids and staff. I worried about them. But they were not the targets. And we all knew it.

Everyone was worried about me. They didn't want me walking through the parking lot alone.

They didn't want me speaking in public. They didn't want my schedule announced to anyone.

The building I drove up to was now fenced and gated.

What was my job becoming?

Was my job working with kids? Or was my job installing security systems to keep dangerous people from blowing my head off? Or was my job facing white supremacists who hated Jews? Or was my job helping a person who wasn't on staff at Cocoon walk through her trauma triggers? Or was my job finding money to fix problems I didn't create? Or was my job ticking off forms and boxes all day for federal grants? Or reading the child protection reports made each day? Or reviewing our training manuals? Searching for money? Helping every kid get an education, which involved closing our on-site school because the government was mandating that public schools pick up kids who were homeless and keep them in school? Or finding a researcher to create a tool to track whether every kid gained independent living skills, employment skills and an education, and, if necessary, recovered from addiction? Was it my job to wear a bulletproof vest?

It no longer felt like my job was working with kids. And I had to be honest: that was the only reason I worked for Cocoon House. For the kids and staff. I loved them.

But being an administrator was also taking me away from them and away from myself.

38

SPIRITUAL SEEKING

The work of Cocoon House was painful. Watching teens who had been abused, neglected and homeless, who struggled with mental health issues, grief and abandonment, was jabbing my soul.

When I lay on my futon at night, I could feel the grief I carried for the kids at Cocoon sinking my body. I whispered their names as prayers. I tried imagining a cloud of safety around each one, filled with light. But then I still cried as I imagined them, one by one. So many kids.

I longed for the spiritual comfort I'd found years ago at a bookstore in Los Angeles called The Bodhi Tree.

I tried meditation. Tempel was often telling me stories at the shelter about how meditation helped him. I could sit quietly with my eyes closed, but the emotional pain still stalked me.

Tempel encouraged me to go to a five-day meditation retreat to hear lectures. And get what? I didn't know. A soothing presence from within was what I hoped for. Maybe the meditation would be more soothing if I were contained in a bubble. The spiritual bubble of a meditation center sounded like a good idea.

The meditation center in Oregon was on top of a mountain. It took hours to drive to it. When I walked in to register, I felt disoriented. The austerity and emptiness were spacious, but inside of me, the spaciousness was filled with pain. It rushed forward like the Skagit River rushes over the banks in a snow melt.

I felt like an outsider. Everyone was wearing slip-off shoes; I was wearing lace-up sneakers. Everyone whispered. Most were silent. People looked at each other with familiarity. They were touching with their eyes. Sexuality was overt. This confused me. People were hooking up in their linen pants, sandals and flowing pullovers. They assigned me a room to myself, which I was grateful for. Everyone seemed to know where they were going, and I needed a map. I was given a schedule and told to listen for the bell for meals.

I dropped my backpack in my room: a twin bed, paneled wood walls, a lamp, a small dresser with two drawers. It was enough.

We gathered into a long line to get a bowl of oatmeal or rice. Everyone was dressed in soft beige and pale colors. It was definitely a style, like they all shopped in the same store. I was the only one in jeans. An obvious outsider.

Between the silence, the bareness and the simplicity of the food, a feeling of deprivation overcame me. I didn't need more deprivation.

I worked in a shelter surrounded by true deprivation; I wasn't sure I needed to be in artificial deprivation. I was suspicious. Tank Girl was asking what the hell we were doing here: "This doesn't look like fun."

I went to the meditation lectures and found sitting rigid with my back straight and legs crossed to be unbearable after 45 minutes. How would I do five full days of that? I stopped attending the meditation lectures in the large hall; I stopped sitting and walked. I wandered into the field of flowers, wearing headphones, listening to Bruce Springsteen's "Thunder Road." Maybe I was dancing, throwing my arms about and air-playing the guitar with Bruce, then rat-a-tat-tatting with Max on the drums, blowing all the air out of my chest with Clarence on sax. I felt the freedom of my college days, singing along with Bruce and thousands of others in a dim stadium.

I am not sure how this was noticed, but it was. Weren't they all in the meditation hall? I was asked to meet with someone in charge, like being hauled into the principal's office for smoking in the girls' locker room. They'd caught me dancing.

There are no written rules about this, but the person in charge sat in a large room on a meditation cushion elevated on a platform. He had me sit on a cushion on the floor below him. I expected a spiritual conversation. Instead, I was kicked out of the meditation retreat center. The loving-kindness teacher asked me to leave in the middle of the night so other attendees wouldn't notice – never mind how I would navigate a road wrapped around a mountain with no lights at night.

Tears streamed down my face as I drove. I wasn't sure where to go. I was disoriented from a few days of silence. I was carrying so much emotional pain; it was unbearable for me to sit in silence with all of it.

The five-day meditation retreat wasn't designed to hold all the pain. I had to pack it up and carry it with me.

I felt lost driving off the mountain and lost inside. I was trying to find my way home, spiritually. I called my girlfriend Valerie. She was a soothing voice, a friend, someone who knew me. She made me laugh. Helped me see how absurd it was and reminded me that I wasn't completely lost. She was, in that moment, an anchor.

Though I was a retreat failure, I longed for some spiritual scaffolding to lean against. I wanted to talk to someone with a spiritual perspective about my experiences. I wanted to talk with people who were spiritually conscious. I believed I was having a spiritual experience and needed help understanding it.

I reached out for my Jewish roots, trying to pull them up from where they were buried in the ground. I was Jewish, not Buddhist. Maybe my own traditions could help me find my way. But I wanted spiritual comfort, and my experience of Judaism wasn't one of comfort. The traditions and stories I learned growing up were of fighting, wars, slavery and people fleeing antisemitism around the globe, for hundreds and hundreds of years. It was a religion with a lot of grief. My family didn't fit the mold of Jewish families. Jewish families didn't abandon their children as my parents had done. I wasn't sure if I'd fit in. My family experience was so different from other Jewish families.

I started meeting with Rabbi David at the synagogue, a temple made from a house in Everett. I spent one lunch break each week with Rabbi David. Though I didn't feel I measured up as religious, I was Jewish. They had to accept me: can't throw me out of Judaism, I was Batmitzvah'd.

From him I learned that walking into the pain of the world was part of Judaism. He explained the Hebrew words *tikun olam* meant repairing the world. It was the soul of the religion. Jewish people were asked to walk into the pain of the world and work on repair. He said I could skip the other rituals and just continue to walk the path of repairing something in the world. He would walk through the pain with me. We met over a period of several months.

I continued meditating on my own, as it seemed it couldn't hurt. It was hard to sit with all the pain, but I also needed to acknowledge it was there. I didn't want to ignore it. My friend Tempel felt bad that I was a retreat failure. He couldn't understand why the meditation teacher had such a strong reaction. He wanted me to try a conversation with spiritual teacher and author Pema Chodron. She was in Seattle. He went to great lengths to arrange a private meeting for me.

I met her in a very austere room. It was clean and empty. There were two chairs, a table, some books in the bookcase. She was wearing a nun's robe. Her head was shaved. I felt overly ornamented and not in her tribe; I also didn't feel like I was moving toward her lifestyle or practice. I met with her because her writing was touching. I had one question for her. But it was the most important spiritual question I had.

"What is spirituality?"

I expected her to give me a complicated answer.

She said, "Spirituality is one thing. It is how you live your life."

That was the answer I needed to hear.

It was consistent with what Rabbi David was teaching me.

It was what The General said too.

I finally understood: Cocoon House was spiritual work for me.

I could accept that pain came with this spiritual work. I worried about the staff and how they were carrying the pain. I wasn't sure what to offer them.

I reached out to Dr. Paul from the Everett Clinic for training on vicarious trauma for the Cocoon staff. I told him how painful the work was – bonding to kids; witnessing their pain; listening to their stories, often of abuse; forming attachments; having to say goodbye; always wondering if a kid would be okay when they left us.

Our staff team gathered to hear Dr. Paul talk about trauma and vicarious trauma, to which we were all vulnerable. He gave out a list of symptoms. The list filled a page. I read down the list, thinking about the staff, thinking about how vulnerable the whole team was to this list. Quietly realizing I had many symptoms.

I sank into my chair. I understood why I was searching for spiritual help. I had vicarious trauma, secondary trauma.

I was ashamed. People who work with traumatized kids are supposed to be able to handle it. The trauma had burst through Tank Girl. Was she the part of me that was tough enough to handle all the trauma, or was she a result of the trauma?

I knew I needed to heal. But it would take time. And this wasn't the right time for me to leave Cocoon House and go on some healing personal journey. The new building wasn't stable, financially or philosophically. We were creating a model for long-term care. We had lots still to figure out, to grow into a long-term housing program that offered what the kids needed.

I was bargaining. I wanted to believe I could stay at Cocoon while I healed my soul. I knew instinctively that writing was what I needed. It was for me a way to listen to my soul.

Writing is different from meditation. I didn't have to sit in silence and hold the pain – I could put it to the page. The paper was a container to hold my feelings.

I didn't yet know that I needed to leave Cocoon House. I didn't know that I needed to stop working with traumatized and abused kids. I didn't know that my soul needed a rest from all the trauma. I didn't know that stopping would be the only way to heal.

I thought doing something would help. If I did more self-care. If I joined a frisbee team. If I spent more time volunteering in my daughters' classes. If I wrote, attended writing workshops. If I meditated.

These things helped. I didn't know that I needed more. I needed more of me. Cocoon House was a job that kept growing. It needed more and more of me, and there wasn't much left. What was left was hurting. Like burnt toast, no one wanted those parts. Tank Girl, she was tough and kept going. "Just go forward," she'd say. But when I looked into her eyes, she was vacant. A mirage. She could keep going, but I couldn't go with her. She was funny and strong, but I had so many more feelings. I couldn't surrender any more of me to be what Cocoon House needed.

I had reached my capacity.

Eventually, I had to accept that I would need to leave Cocoon House to do more of my own healing. I knew it wasn't some spiritual shortcoming; I accepted that I had secondary trauma. But I held my secondary trauma as a secret for a while.

I would work to make Cocoon strong, very strong, so it could withstand anything, including my leaving. I too had to become stronger. Strong enough to let go.

39

SECONDARY TRAUMA

Secondary trauma is like being at the bottom of a deep canyon, alone, without a way out. You know that trying to climb out of the canyon will kill you and staying will kill you. I stared at the list of symptoms on secondary trauma; it was a map without directions. What was I supposed to do with all this?

Tank Girl, the part of me that is always strong and fearless, reviewed the list.

"Don't worry about this," she said. "It's for the staff – not you."

I stared trance-like at the list of symptoms. "What happens when I am the one with secondary trauma?"

Tank Girl was cocky and confident. "We can kick this. Just play more frisbee, do whatever the hell makes you feel good. You know how it works."

I was already doing things that made me feel good.

Tank Girl was pacing back and forth in her green army pants with the strawberry patch and black T-shirt.

"Get me a cigarette!"

I don't smoke anymore.

Tank Girl didn't want to deal with this "secondary trauma shit."

It was hard enough the first time through post-traumatic stress disorder (PTSD). Back to the list of symptoms. I folded it up and put in my purse.

"Let's just toss that in the trash!" barked Tank Girl.

I put it in my file cabinet. Then I stole it from the file cabinet and folded it up smaller and carried it in my pocket like an amulet.

But the little piece of paper did not protect me.

"You can kick this," Tank Girl said. "Go to the doctor. He'll fix you right up. He'll tell you THERE IS NOTHING WRONG with you." She rolled her eyes at me.

I returned to my doctor. I was nauseous and tired – so tired I couldn't climb a flight of stairs.

At the doctor's office, he left my medical record in a manila folder on the table. Of course I opened it. The file contained the last ten years of my life. I opened and scanned the page. It said EXHAUSTION in large letters, taking up half the page with three exclamation marks. I flipped to the next page. EXHAUSTION. Next page: "Once again, she is exhausted."

This file went back ten years. The word "exhausted" was on every page.

I had been going round and round in circles for ten years, getting exhausted, hoping my doctor would prop me up to just keep going.

When my doctor asked how I felt, I didn't know how to tell him. Where would I begin?

"How are things going at Cocoon House?" he asked. His office was only a few miles away. He was a supporter of the organization. "Everything going well there?"

I couldn't find words. No words at all.

"Things are fine," blurted Tank Girl. "I'm just tired."

I wanted to lie down on the exam table and take a nap. Just 20–30 minutes. I laid down and shut my eyes.

"GET UP!!" It was Tank Girl. She was not having this.

I am certain my visit ended with my doctor telling me I needed to rest. But I didn't know how to rest.

It's a simple word. But I had no idea how to stop and rest.

I drank more coffee.

Symptom one from the list of symptoms of secondary trauma: Exhaustion.

Cocoon House always had something going on. No sooner did I handle one drama, a new one took center stage. There was always a fire to put out, and if I wasn't putting out a fire, I knew it was just a matter of days or moments before the next one. Tank Girl was always on the prowl.

I carried a black pager on my hip 24 hours a day for seven years in a row. No matter what happened, I was responsible for it.

Symptom 2: Hypervigilance.

I always had a worry in the back of my mind, and guilt that I wasn't doing enough. If I made a mistake, we could be closed down. I was a crow sitting over her eggs. I couldn't leave my nest; I was responsible. I had to do everything better than perfect. I had to excel at every single grant table.

Symptoms 3, 4, and 5: Guilt, fear, sleeplessness.

After dealing with the sprinkler system at the new building, our architect was doing a walkthrough and asked what I thought of the second-floor improvements. I hadn't looked. I had too much to deal with on my desk to go upstairs and look around. I could only care about so much.

He had to drag me away from my desk to go upstairs.

Symptom 6: A loss of interest in things.

At first, I could only be with my feelings in dark, quiet places. I went to the movies in the middle of the day. No one would be in the theater – just me. And as the lights went down, I cried. I cried and cried for as long as I needed to. Then, when the movie was over, I collected myself and left.

Instead of a workout at the gym, I went straight to the sauna. Shut off the light. Sat on my towel trying to sweat the emotional pain out of my body.

Symptoms 7 and 8: Profound sadness and hiding feelings.

I felt so much shame around having secondary trauma. How could this happen to me? I was supposed to be an executive director, a psychotherapist and a leader. How could I lead and crumble?

I was crumbling.

Secondary trauma was bringing me to my knees.

Understanding secondary trauma did not protect me from it. Sure, I knew what it was. I watched out for all the staff as part of my 24 hours a day on call, making sure they were not being brought to their knees.

Every staff member was flammable, like clothing near a lit candle. We were witnessing pain and trauma every day. I could see when staff members were showing signs: long, breathy sighs; rings under eyes from not sleeping; being unusually quiet; avoiding conversations; recurring colds and coughing.

I would give them time off to heal. As long as they needed. We talked about a care plan they would follow. I would hold their job until they could come back. I always held their job. There was no judgement. I didn't want to replace people because they got sick from the exposure to their feelings.

The job at Cocoon brought up feelings. I wanted caring people who would bring their hearts to work. When you bring your heart to work, you are flammable.

One minute it was a sunny spring day, and I was carrying my coffee and saying good morning to the staff and kids. The next minute I was taking a call from the hospital that a kid we all knew was hit on his bicycle in the middle of the night. He died at the scene. He was trying to get away from his drunk father. He was 12 years old.

Though we were all doing as much as we could to help, we couldn't save everyone. And when our beds were full, we turned kids away.

Symptom 9: Helplessness.

For many years, this tough exterior that everyone saw in me, Tank Girl, covered my own flammability.

I knew I had underlying PTSD from my childhood. Though I had processed it, gone to therapy and healed, I knew PTSD never fully leaves. There is a trail inside of me that leads back to it. I could travel up the trail and be away from it and symptom-free . . . but life has trauma triggers. And when I was triggered, symptoms of PTSD returned.

And I was in a job that was triggering all the time. I had been ignoring my own feelings, ignoring that I was sitting in dark movie theaters crying. Ignoring that, I went to a writing retreat; all I could produce on the page were tears. I was flammable.

Symptom 10: A vulnerability to secondary trauma because of past PTSD.

I realized Tank Girl helped me fight the battles I fought for Cocoon House. She was battle-ready, dealing with state laws – a huntress, relentless in the search for whatever Cocoon needed.

But she couldn't help me when I wasn't fighting.

I was hiding my vulnerability from everyone, but I could no longer hide it from myself.

Tank Girl was ashamed of me. She kicked me and yelled at me. I had disappointed her. "You are a failure, the worst therapist in the world," she howled.

She wanted me to make this disappear. She was using spirituality to dissolve the pain I was in.

Longer meditations, more books, more conversations with the Rabbi. Attempting a meditation retreat.

I didn't have the words to say, "I can't sit with this pain."

"I can't sit in silence without crying."

"I need something else."

When I left the meditation center alone, I knew it was a symbolic moment.

I needed to leave Cocoon House.

Just thinking those words made my head split like a tree hit by lightning.

Wasn't leaving Cocoon House abandonment?

Abandonment was the very thing I was trying never to do in my life.

I was standing at a threshold. I realized that ignoring all my symptoms of secondary trauma was also abandonment.

I could not abandon myself any longer.

I wasn't in a minor, early stage of secondary trauma. It was severe. I could no longer taste my food. I could only feel if I was having sex.

I was ashamed that I had become so ill. The little folded piece of paper I carried everywhere with me was my flag, my poem, my courage. My reminder that I had to save myself.

I told the people who were closest to me. It wasn't a big public thing, just my inner circle. I didn't want to keep hiding this. I needed time off. I needed to stop working with abused kids. I needed to leave Cocoon House.

40

WILL LEAVING

Lilly came into my office carrying a fat photo album. She curled up in a chair and read aloud a letter from a family wanting to adopt a child. She held up the book to show me the photo of the family.

"They look nice."

There must have been more than 60 families in the photo album. I wondered how she would pick a family. How does anyone pick a family?

Maybe this family looked like the family she would have liked to be in. She chose three families to meet with. I told her if she didn't like those three, she could meet others.

She wanted an open adoption. Kim was by her side through every single step of the process.

After meeting with five families, she found the family for Will. After meetings in the park, a trip to their home and a counseling session, it was time for baby Will to leave and go to his new family. I couldn't picture in my head, how it would go when baby Will would be picked up by "the family." Would they hand Lilly flowers as a thank-you while she handed them her child? Would Will cry as he was carried out the door with strangers? No, that wouldn't happen. The family were not strangers. Will had been around them a few times. Will was used to being carried around by different people, taken out for pediatrician visits in unfamiliar cars, going off to the Happy Baby Daycare Center at the high school when Lilly went to class.

No, Will probably wouldn't be crying as they carried him away. It was just another set of loving, trusted hands around him. Will wouldn't know that this was his last time going through the doors of Cocoon – the only place Will had known as a home. Will wouldn't know that he was not returning to his crib in room 214. Will wouldn't know that he would not be waking up to his mommy ever again – that he was going to learn to call a new person "Mommy."

And what about Lilly? Would Lilly just explode into a thousand pieces as they carried Will out the door? How would we put her back together again? Yes, she wanted this adoption, but could she imagine not carrying Will around on her right hip? Could she imagine feeding just herself and not have Will in the highchair beside her? Could she imagine room 214 without a crib?

After sending Lilly to parenting classes for a full year to prepare her how to care for Will, had we done anything to prepare her for not having Will?

I felt like I was waking up from a nightmare, the kind where you have forgotten the thing you need the most. I wanted to run into Cocoon Complex and yell, "Wait, stop! Everyone freeze! We are not ready to send Will off with 'the family.' We forgot the most important part! We haven't gotten Lilly ready for this, for today, for the door closing and Will being driven away. We haven't talked about the crib that is still in Lilly's room or the highchair in the kitchen. And what about the toys? Would Lilly get to keep something that was Will's? Or does Will need all his stuffies?"

I put my hand on my heart. "Try to hold it together," I whispered to myself and ran through the rooms of Cocoon looking for Kim. I wanted to ask Kim, Lilly's person, "How are we all going to survive this?"

I found Kim with Lilly on the second floor. Lilly's door was open. Kim was folding Will's baby clothes with Lilly. Kim held up a shirt with a bear; she and Lilly broke into laughter.

Kim said, "I will never forget when we were trying this on him in Target, and he vomited right down the front of it." Kim could hardly get the words out, she was laughing so hard. Lilly chimed in, "That checkout dude! Remember him?"

Then Kim stood up, exhaled, looked at Lilly, waved the teddy bear shirt and said, "Keep or pack ?"

Lilly said, "It doesn't fit him anymore. Donate it."

"Okay, Kim and Lilly have this," I thought. Whatever this awful process was, Kim was with Lilly sorting through it, one piece at a time.

"Hey, where's Will?" I asked.

"He's in the kitchen with Sabina," said Lilly.

Then Lilly added, "Do you want to give him a last hug?"

Was I still breathing? I wasn't sure. Could I walk downstairs? I looked down at my legs to see if they were still attached to my body. "Last hug" pummeled me.

"Yeah, I'll go see him in the kitchen and get my hugs in."

I walked into the kitchen. Sabina had Will on her hip. Several staff who weren't on shift were also in the kitchen. A group of teens were at the table, drawing on a large sheet of white butcher-block paper.

I stroked Will's curly black hair. He reached his pudgy arms out to me.

Sabina looked at me and pouted. I knew she didn't want to hand him off. But I smiled at Will and lifted him onto my chest and right hip. "How's my baby butterfly?"

I kissed the top of his head and inhaled his hair above his ear. He smelled like cookies.

Sabina had a tray out for the teens.

"What are all the kids doing out of school at 10:30?" I asked.

Sabina said, "They're making a goodbye card. We're having a goodbye party. The kids all wanted to be here when the family comes." They were all home sick from school.

"That makes sense," I thought. Of course. It wasn't only Lilly saying goodbye to her son. Will was like a cousin or baby brother to all the other kids.

My stomach heaved for all the other kids. What would it be like for them? My nightmare returned. Did we forget to prepare all the other kids? How would we do that now? I squeezed into a spot on the bench where the kids were drawing a goodbye card. I sat Will on my knee. He reached for a marker.

"Oh, let's make something on this!" said Angel. Thin, hair trimmed very close to his head, with black skin that glowed under pink lashes glued to his eyelids, Angel was our resident artist. He had a fake diamond in his nose piercing, and loose, striped bell-bottom pants he'd made himself.

Angel always had creative ideas.

I put the marker in Will's hand. He waved it in the air – not quite to the paper. I gently wrapped my hand around his, and we landed on the goodbye paper. I opened my hand and watched him make a squiggle on the page. He lifted his hand in the air, and I put the cap on the marker.

The door opened to our dining hall, and Tempel and Danny came in. One was carrying a tile, and the other was carrying a bag of rust-colored clay.

"Hi, Willy-Nilly!" said Tempel with a big smile.

He put a rust-colored lump of clay on the table. "Can I have him?"

"Sure." I passed him Will.

He slipped the marker out of his hand. "I'm going to need both your hands."

And he sat Will on his lap and plunged both his little hands into the clay.

The kids stopped drawing. "Oh, I want one!" The kids were all swaying toward Tempel.

He looked at the bag of clay and said, "Take some."

All the kids were passing the bag of clay and grabbing a lump, pressing it on the table to make it flat and then handing the square to Tempel to press Will's hands.

I put my hand on Tempel's shoulder and squeezed.

"Great idea," I whispered.

I felt tears welling up. I got up to go back to my office, room 110. I walked across the courtyard wondering if I would be able to watch the kids say goodbye. The kids were watching Will get something none of them had: a family.

I sat at my desk and looked out the window onto the courtyard. Lilly and Kim had come downstairs and were crossing the grass into the kitchen. Lilly, dressed in fleece pajama pants and slippers, carried a bag and a laundry basket of toys. Kim had an armful of clothes.

I thought about the idea of family. How was Lilly able to give Will something she never had?

I got up off my seat to go back to the kitchen. I knew what was going to happen. I could see it now clearly. We were all going to be in the kitchen together. We would watch as the tiniest piece of our Cocoon family went to his new home.

Right on time, the family came through the door: the mom, the dad, and they had two little boys with them. Will would get two brothers. One was four and one was six. Lilly pulled little gift-wrapped boxes out of her bag and bent over to hand a present to each of the little boys.

I looked at Kim. She whispered, "Her idea."

The parents hugged Lilly. The mom handed Lilly a photo album. She said, "These are all pictures from our visits to the park, the day at the zoo and the beach." She hugged Lilly and said, "There will be many more days and visits together." Lilly held the photo album to her chest and said, "Thank you." Tears were streaming down her face.

She let out an exhale, wiped her face with her sleeve and turned around to the teens at the table.

"Hey, come on, y'all. It's time to say goodbye." The kids got up. Angel and Leroy folded the big card and they handed it to the dad.

"This way when he's older he'll have something to remember us." Leroy said. He looked down at his shoes and said, "Take good care of him."

Angel stepped back to lean into the wall. I wanted to do the same thing.

Each kid rubbed their hands on Will's head, gave him a hug or squeezed his hand, kissed his cheek. Sabina came out of the kitchen and wiped her hands on her apron. She wiped tears from her eyes and then she rubbed Will's back.

I went last. I put my hands on his head one last time and closed my eyes. I wanted to send him out into the world with a blessing.

"May you always be loved," I whispered.

Lilly asked Kim to gather up the things.

Then she said out loud, "Okay, y'all, it's time."

The family stood there. The four-year-old reached around his mom's leg. The family didn't move. The family didn't know what to do next. We all just stared at each other.

Lilly broke the silence. "It's okay, you can go. Take him." Lilly turned her back away from the door. I put my arm around her shoulder and held her. I too turned away from the door. I heard the door squeak open, and the six-year-old yelled, "Bye!"

The kids and staff muttered, "Bye."

I heard Angel's singsong voice. "So long, farewell . . . ."

The door closed. I pulled Lilly into my chest.

She said, "I'm okay, I'm okay, I'm okay."

Kim bent down and looked up into Lilly's eyes. Kim said, "We got you."

41

LILLY IN THE TULIP FIELDS

I was driving north on I-5. A brief stop at Cocoon House to pick up Lilly. It was a special outing, just Lilly and me on the road north, to take her to see the tulips in bloom. I don't usually take a day alone with one kid from Cocoon. This was an exception.

Lilly had become silent after giving up Will. Her big voice was no longer yelling across the courtyard. I no longer had to put the phone down and tell her to turn down the music while I was talking to a funder. Lilly wasn't even fighting with the staff or slamming doors. It was like she wasn't there.

I was hoping to listen to her talk, the way teenagers do only in a moving car. We were driving north on a Wednesday to avoid the big weekend crowds. Lilly and I would have the fields to ourselves. I hoped the tulip fields would lift her spirits.

The Skagit Valley farms are in bloom once a year, for two weeks. It is a Western Washington ritual to photograph your children, your dogs, your friends, in the middle of the tulip fields. I made the trip each year with Somer and Aliza wearing rain boots to jump in the mud puddles, between the rows of purples, reds, pinks and blazing oranges.

As we drove, Lilly recognized a sign for Mount Vernon.

"I lived there once," she said.

"When was that?" I asked, trying not to push. I knew Lilly's memories would be hard for her, and I didn't want her to land in an apocalypse.

"I lived there with my mom. She was really crazy then. I remember the ambulance. She was bleeding from both wrists."

"I'm sorry, Lilly. What a tough memory. I didn't know you had lived near here."

"I've lived everywhere." Her words were slow and dreamlike. She turned her head away and looked out the car window.

I knew when she looked away, her lips closed, she was drifting away from the car, away from the town.

I didn't want to lose her.

Softly, I tried calling her back.

"Lilly, did you ever see the tulip fields when you lived here?"

She turned back to me.

"No, I don't know what you mean by tulip field. The only thing I remember seeing when I lived here was the hospital where I got to visit my mom."

My heart ached.

I started getting angry with myself. It was a terrible idea to bring Lilly here. It wasn't an uplifting day for her. I'd just stirred up all these awful memories for her. The tulip fields weren't a goddamn band-aid for what she had been through.

But I couldn't just leave her in her bedroom at Cocoon Complex. I didn't want her to be alone, looking at the spot where the crib used to be, walking around the campus without her baby boy in her arms. She had a full year of memories with her son at Cocoon. And she was so quiet. The grief was suffocating her.

I hoped time together, away from the other kids, might be good for her. But really, I had no idea what was good for her. I was just driving us both north.

We turned off the interstate, followed the road over the bridge and saw the tiny signs with arrows: TULIPS. I followed the sign and saw a field of bright purple and red, stretching in wavy ribbons along the valley. I pulled into the muddy parking lot.

Lilly jumped from the car, running across the street to the field of tulips. She was yelling,

"Look at all these fucking flowers!" as her white sneakers sloshed through the mud.

I grabbed my camera and chased after her, shooting pictures of her back, arms outstretched, mud all the way up her calves on her jeans.

I thought, "The staff are going to kill me – wrecking the one pair of shoes she has." I decided I would just stop on our way back and buy her new shoes. The jeans could be washed, at least.

I watched her run up and down first the red rows, then the purple rows. She slowed down and started walking by the time she got to the yellow sections. I watched her. The first smile in weeks, the flat-pancake look on her face was gone. She was laughing.

"Okay, this is why we came," I thought.

I went up to the shack at the edge of the field and bought us tea and tulip-shaped cookies. I sat at the one bench set up by the field. Now and then, she turned her head toward me to make sure I was still there. I waved to her.

Lilly wore herself out running up and down the rows. She yelled, "Can I get a cookie?" I waved her cookie in the air.

She returned breathless and hurled herself down on the bench.

She looked up eating her cookie, her eyes following the tree above, an umbrella shape hanging over us.

She reached for the leaves and ran them through her fingers.

"What kind of tree is this?"

Tears welled up in my eyes. She didn't know. "Oh god," I thought. "Of all the places to put the one and only bench. How did I not notice this?"

I finally said, "It's a weeping willow."

She smiled and tears rolled down her face. She reached both hands through the chains of leaves.

I put my arms around her as she cried into my shoulder. After a minute, she pushed herself off me and stood back. She looked me in the eye. Her brown eyes were flat, the pancake look back on her face.

"I want you to promise me something."

"Sure. What?"

"I'm going to stay at Cocoon until I am grown up. 'Til I am 18. Will you promise me you will stay at Cocoon until I am grown up?"

Oh, what a promise. She couldn't bear another ending.

Kids that came and went from Cocoon. Staff that came and went. When we started our drive, I didn't know what Lilly needed. And now she was telling me.

She needed someone to stay. And to stay for her.

I got up and hugged her.

"Yes, I will stay until you leave."

We returned to Cocoon Complex. She grabbed a black marker pen from my car console and, as we walked into the building, she pulled the cap off the marker and wrote her name on the wall of the building.

Right in front of me. Unafraid of authority. Knowing darn well I would let her get away with it.

Every fear I had that we would lose Lilly to the streets left my body in one long exhale. I looked at her name in permanent marker on the building.

Lilly was staying put.

42

LEAVING COCOON HOUSE

Endings have always felt like long marches through dark tunnels. Every ending brings up the very first experience of an ending – that little girl in the courtroom, losing my parents and my home. Endings forever after were perilous, hurling me into night terrors.

I learned along the way how to prepare for goodbyes, how to get out of bed and leave the night terrors. I reminded myself it would end. I would get through it. Cocoon House was born right out of my hip, named in my dreams. It shaped who I was over ten years, as much as I shaped it.

The community surrounding Cocoon House became a family to me. It taught me what family really was. For all my searching and joining other families, there was a sense of deep commitment with Cocoon. The kind of commitment families make to each other.

How could I step away from it?

The seed of my leaving Cocoon started two years earlier. I knew when I promised Lilly I would stay that I would leave after Lilly turned 18.

Now, she had her GED in her hand, her butterfly medal, a recipe book from Sabina and her 18th birthday party. She had work experience. She had pictures of her son, letters from the family. She was ready to move on. Her plan was to visit her mom, who was living in a group home. Lilly got her train ticket, and we said goodbye. My promise was kept.

I'd known I would be leaving one day, feeling the same uncertainty as an 18-year-old, trying to imagine that future.

My work at Cocoon continued after Lilly left.

I was working with the other local housing agencies on a presentation about families and teens entering different shelters. My part of the presentation was to photograph all the different local shelters. I went out with my camera and looked inside the nook and crannies we called "shelter." There were small signs of children and babies everywhere in the shelters, a bottle half-filled, a doll on a bed with a ragged haircut, a game with worn box edges on a table, a pile of bibs and diapers on a shelf.

My camera was making me look at many things I hadn't considered before. Why were there so many children in the family shelters? Why didn't they have books and toys? Why wasn't there carpeting for babies to crawl on? Why weren't there highchairs?

I blew up the photographs to eight-by-ten size and carried them in my tote bag every day.

Sometimes I would pull out the photographs and stare at them as I drank my coffee.

I had no idea why I was carrying these pictures with me.

Then one day, randomly, I got a call from The General. Ever since he'd written that check paying for our sprinkler system, he and I had met for lunch a few times a year. I was always eager to hear his wisdom, and I had no idea what he got out of meeting with me other than usually a very entertaining story or two. Now he called to say he was passing through Everett. Would I meet him for coffee?

We were seated in a Starbucks on Colby Avenue at a small round table. I remember the *shhhhh* of the espresso machine, the acoustic music playing over the speakers in the background. The General was in a tailored suit. He stood out in the room with a hipster reading, a mom and toddler with a stroller, and two women interviewing someone. I was in my simple black pants and solid-colored shirt.

I sipped my coffee and confessed that I would be leaving Cocoon House sometime in the upcoming year.

I asked, "Will you and the Medina Foundation continue supporting Cocoon House if someone else is running it?"

"Of course. But why are you thinking about leaving?"

I wanted to tell him the truth. He was a General. He knew what PTSD was. I wanted to be honest with someone.

"I have secondary trauma. It's all these abused kids over so many years. I need time off to heal."

"Why can't the board give you a sabbatical for a year?"

"For one thing, I haven't told my board. The board would do that in a heartbeat. But I don't honestly know how long it will take for me to heal. And I don't think this is the job for me any longer. Cocoon needs someone who wants to be an administrator. That's not really what I am. I am a people person. I work with people. I need to recover and then do that."

Then he asked, "So, what would you do if you were given a million dollars?"

"Really? We are going to imagine this?" I laughed.

He waited. "No, really, if you were given a million dollars, no strings attached, what would you do?"

I guess he thought I'd say I'd go off to a tropical island. But that is not what came up for me.

"If I had a million dollars, I would do something about this." I pulled out the photos of the shelters from my tote bag.

He was stunned. It isn't easy to stun the General.

I spread the photos across the coffee table. He looked closely at the photos of dismal-looking rooms, bedsheets hung across windows at the women's shelter, a small twin bed with a toy on it where a family of three was sleeping nightly in a family shelter. A kitchen that had three chairs, one with a broken leg, in a shelter that served families. Four babies in residence and no highchair. No carpet on the floor for crawling. No play rooms. No desks for homework.

"If I had a million dollars, I would change this. All these little children are going through the adult shelters, and they're not set up for kids. I checked the stats; two-thirds of the people in shelters are little kids!"

"What could a million dollars get you?" He gazed over the pictures, holding them up one at a time to the light.

Making it up in the moment, I said, "A million dollars could get a three-year demonstration project. I'd work with a group of housing agencies to create supports across the housing system for children. Once we have the model figured out, it could be replicated."

Our coffee was now cold.

He looked at me said, "Would you bring these photos and present this to the board of our foundation?"

The path in front of me was shifting. A new door was opening in front of me. I knew this opportunity was a one of a kind.

***

Two weeks later, I drove to the exclusive offices of the Medina Foundation. This time I knew the attendant's name in the garage. This time I was wearing a fitted blue suit – something my friend Karla would wear – and patent leather pumps.

I was meeting the board of directors behind one of the largest foundations in Washington State. I started by thanking them. I passed around my photographs. I shared a vision of a three-year demonstration project called One Childhood Lasts a Lifetime.

The foundation board asked many questions. I knew every answer. We weren't going to build an organization. This would be a model. We'd show other foundations how to fund supports for the kids in these shelters. We'd break the cycle in families.

The Medina Foundation funded all three years of the project.

In order to do this, though, I needed to leave Cocoon House. The project did not involve any personal work with homeless and abused kids. I would be one step removed and work with those who were doing the work. It would give me three years away from direct trauma and give me time to heal.

I had to tell my own board. I asked the Medina Foundation to hold off on announcing this million-dollar grant award, at the time one of the largest startup awards ever made in the United States.

I said, "Please wait. My board, my staff, we need time together to absorb this before it is public."

Cocoon House was strong. Cocoon had funding for the next three years in the bank. It was no longer a wobbling, uncertain nonprofit. It was no longer breathing from my lungs.

Cocoon was standing on solid ground between two buildings. We had a philosophy of care that was working for teens. And the organization would continue doing its work without me.

As an organization, we learned how to help a kid get off the streets.

We had "institutional knowledge," from getting to know our teens, having relationships with them, studying trauma and research, and trying things – listening to kids and letting them lead.

Experience.

Institutional knowledge can only be earned. It can't be bought or awarded. Ours was earned one kid at a time.

Cocoon House was finally there.

When I was ready to tell my board, we took our time with my exit. My board created a beautiful ceremony, a ten-year celebration of Cocoon House and a time for me to say goodbye.

Tim, the volunteer who took charge of all the repairs year in and year out, invited me to the stage to give my final goodbye.

Notes from the Ten-Year Celebration of Cocoon

Making closure, saying goodbye, just doesn't come easy for me. So, if you missed the beautiful article that was in the Herald when I announced my resignation, and if you missed my three-page goodbye letter, and if you missed the parties where I was completely speechless at Cocoon Complex and Wicked Cellar, this is it. This is the public family closure. But today I am ready. And I'm not speechless.

And this moment in the event is my butterfly speech. At Cocoon, a butterfly speech means goodbye.

I hope what comes through to you today, through this event, is what Cocoon House means. I hope you leave here with your heart pierced; then, you will understand how it felt for me each day at Cocoon.

Cocoon House was not a job, it was and is a place. Work, jobs, tasks happen in that place.

But it is not "what that place is."

There is a belief that what we name things – the words we call things, the names we give to others – carries an energy and can be prophetic.

Every day, every hour, every year, Cocoon House lived up to its name.

It is a place of transformation.

Today, when we give medals to the kids, you will hear some of them talk about the big transformations they've made. But not so obvious to you, will be that Cocoon was a place of transformation not just for the kids, but for every person who ever worked there.

And that included me.

A place of transformation.

Inside of the word "transformation" is a smaller word, one that fits between my hands: "formation." Formation is the doing part of transformation.

I was part of birthing Cocoon House. It first formed inside my head as an idea. But the idea would only have been an idea without the help from most of you in the room today.

Big visions, dreams, ideas are not "formed"– literally, they are without form.

Unless people give them shape.

"Trans" – to cross over, to say goodbye.

Over the ten years of running Cocoon, I grew up. I went from being a young, wise, thinner 29-year-old, to a 40-year-old. I carried my twin babies nearly everywhere I went as I developed the agency. I look back on those moments today, and I admire that young woman.

> *My message to the young people in this room today is: Don't look for the hero outside of you.*
>
> *Don't look for the superstar, the celebrity, the king of the world.*
>
> *Look for yourself.*
>
> *Find the hero inside of you and be that hero.*

I look a final look around the room, the hundreds of people there. My beloved board members Geoff, Mary Lou, Lyle; Karla, my ally from the Teen Advocates; Jeri Costa; Kim; Chief; California Ted; Tim, Jim and all the Lions; the General; and so many others. Out of the corner of my eye, I saw my dad. My board had flown him in as a surprise. They kept him sequestered in a hotel and had him seated in the back of the room for what I can only call my butterfly ceremony.

I was surrounded by so much love from the community, the staff, the kids, the windows and walls, the trees and garden. I felt love everywhere. Leaving all that love is what made it a different ending.

I learned from Cocoon to make loving goodbyes.

The final thing I did, eight days before leaving Cocoon House, was to meet with the Lions. I handed them a check to buy the shelter house in full. Cocoon House no longer needed to rent the space for $10 a month.

This time it was the Lions who were surprised. I explained they could now use the bingo parlor they mortgaged to make another incredible community investment.

43

PLUM VILLAGE

"Within us is a true home, indestructible."
Dharma talk, Plum Village

Bordeaux, France
Seventeen years after leaving Cocoon House

My friend Linda arrived in the darkness of early morning, her car
loaded with a picnic basket, a red-and-white thermos of hot tea,
two ceramic mugs, a blanket for my legs and, most importantly, the
directions to Plum Village.

If Santa and the North Pole were the haven for my child-mind,
Thich Nhat Hanh's Plum Village in France was the refuge for my
adult mind. It was the one place on earth I knew I had to visit in
this lifetime. He wrote about Plum Village in his book, *The Sun of
My Heart.*

I first began reading Thich Nhat Hanh's words in The Bodhi Tree
Bookstore when I was in my 20s. The Bodhi Tree in Los Angeles was
a refuge. This jewel of a bookstore was where I began my spiritual
seeking, looking for something calming and soothing from the terrible
pain of my family.

I'd come to that bookstore often – sometimes to get away from
the phone calls from my troubled family, sometimes to get away from
myself. I came with one question. The question weighed on me and
was mine to carry: How would I heal?

Thirty-five years later, I was on my way to Plum Village, a place established by Thich Nhat Hanh. Knowing I was going to be in France and within a short distance of Plum Village, I emailed to ask if I could visit. A few weeks later, I received an invitation to Plum Village.

The invitation was for a Dharma talk at 9:30am in Plum Village. Linda had taken on the assignment of driving as a spiritual mission. I felt like I was sitting beside an angel driving the car. She had one focus, determined to get us to Plum Village for the Dharma talk. She estimated we'd arrive an hour early. We sped down the narrow roads, winding among hills, vineyards, chateaus, climbing ever higher as the roads narrowed ever tighter. We kept losing our sense of direction and place. Through a combination of guessing and many U-turns, we saw orange signs to Plum Village. It was ten minutes before the scheduled talk. The parking lot was eerie and empty, and I was certain something was wrong. We couldn't be the only ones invited to the talk. As we made our way past beautiful empty halls, we finally saw two people. I hesitated to speak to them, knowing it is not nice etiquette to interrupt silence at a meditation center. I let Linda ask. She didn't know the etiquette.

"Which way is the Dharma talk for 9:30?"

The couple looked at us bewildered. The Dharma talk was not at this Plum Village, it was at the other Plum Village. What?

"There is more than one. Yes, there are three hamlets."

I didn't even know what a hamlet was, but we were 20 minutes from the correct Plum Village.

We were certain to be late for the talk.

Linda and I held hands and ran from the wrong hamlet, laughing at how absurd it was to be running out of a Buddhist monastery.

Very unmindful.

But Linda was determined to get us to the right Plum Village entrance.

I put my hand on hers in the car and laughed and said, "It is enough for me to be here. It's okay if we are too late to enter the hall for the talk. It is truly enough just to sit on the grounds and meditate. Your effort, your devotion to getting me here, was enough."

But Linda floored it, and we sped out of the monastery to get to the next hamlet.

We entered the right hamlet and were met by a smiling monk, a huge smile on his face, in a long, brown robe. He welcomed us, bowing, and escorted us to the seats in the hall.

When I took my seat and closed my eyes to breathe and land in my seat in Plum Village, I felt the spirit of my rescue dog, Coco, leap into my arms and lick my face. Her energy somehow found me here. Coco, when I adopted her, had been in a shelter for months, had gone through emergency surgery and was not responding to people. She was half the weight she needed to be. I had never adopted a dog from a shelter, but when I met Coco, she licked my hand, and I knew I needed to bring her home. I nursed her back to health over two years. As she healed, I thought of all the healing I witnessed at Cocoon House and how each kid has a light within them.

I opened my eyes and the monk giving the Dharma talk said, "Within us is a true home, indestructible."

Those were the words, the deeper truth I had been searching for my whole life. Only now, I could feel the truth. I had understood that this was the way of healing trauma. The monk went on to say, "Samsara begins the cycle of well-being." In other words, when we suffer, it leads us to seek our healing.

I spent decades witnessing that truth over and over again, in myself, my grown children, my friends, clients I worked with over time, the teens at Cocoon House and Coco, my little dog. We bend toward the light.

The monk ended the talk by saying, "Buddha is just a continuation of his spiritual ancestors. We are all just a continuation of our ancestors."

That seemed to bring everything more clearly into view: I was a continuation of my ancestors. The immediate mental health issues of the two previous generations in my family set me on my path to search for how we heal. I no longer was hurting and angry at my ancestors. I could send each of them love. I would never have become who I was without them. Because of them, I learned the art of healing. Because of my ancestors, I started Cocoon House. Because of my ancestors, I worked to heal within.

I visited the bookstore near the meditation hall. A young Black woman stood next to me, looking at all the books he had written. Thich Nhat Hanh was now 90; he had written more than 100 books. She was perhaps in her 20s.

"I've never read any of his books," she said. "What would you recommend?" I thought of myself at her age, seeking spiritual comfort. I looked at the shelves, pulled down *Being Peace* and said, "Begin here."

I didn't know about her struggles, her life, why she came to Plum Village, but I hoped she would find healing too.

Then I left the bookshop and stood in Plum Village, feeling Thich That Hahn's words embodied not only in me, but in the trees, the stones, the lotus, the monks, the nuns.

I walked the well-worn walking meditation paths in the garden, green grass flattened by so many feet. It gave me comfort. There are many paths for healing, and they are for all of us. I walked slowly on the path in Plum Village, doing a walking meditation, and as I moved, I heard singing through the trees.

NOTE FROM THE AUTHOR

Thank you to the community that supported Cocoon House. You overwhelmed me with your dedication. I am grateful for the safety net you gave teens who needed us to offer a home and place to grow up.

Cocoon House continues to support youth every single day. You can find out more at cocoonhouse.org.

Cocoon House profoundly changed my life. I recovered from secondary trauma with lots of self-care, boundaries and a commitment to overwhelm recovery. When I healed, I turned my attention to others working in human services, healthcare and education. Today I pass along the gifts of boundaries and overwhelm recovery for those who are serving others. You can find out more on my website, sarrigilman.com

ACKNOWLEDGMENTS

This book has been nurtured by many people at writing workshops and at my kitchen table with dear friends. It would not be in your hands without their encouragement and support. I am grateful to each of them for their time and care, thoughtful notes, feedback, questions, soup, coffee, tea and wisdom. Much appreciation to Rev. Charlene Ray, Tammy Green, Valerie Landsburg, Dr. Deborah Nedelman, Ken Kortlever and Dr. Kathy Burgoyne. They each read this book with love and invested their precious time. I am deeply grateful to each one of them.

Kathy insisted that this book "had to be published" and she reached out to connect me with Trigger Publishing.

Though I carried these stories and wrote them many times, the workshop where it all came together was at Esalen Institute with Katie Hafner. All the final stories to include were voted on by our writing group as this book was crafted. It is an act of generosity to read and give feedback on early shitty drafts. Thank you.

Thank you to Trigger Publishing and Soraya Nair. You are a dream to work with, and I am grateful you embraced this book.

I also want to acknowledge the many significant people who are part of my family, my life and part of Cocoon who are not in this book. I love you. I am grateful for our connection.

ABOUT CHERISH EDITIONS

Cherish Editions is a bespoke publishing service for authors of mental health, well-being and inspirational books.

As a division of Trigger Publishing, the UK's leading independent mental health and well-being publisher, we are experienced in creating and selling positive, responsible, important and inspirational books, which work to de-stigmatize the issues around mental health and improve the mental health and well-being of those who read our titles.

Founded by Adam Shaw, a mental health advocate, author and philanthropist, and leading psychologist Lauren Callaghan, Cherish Editions aims to publish books that provide advice, support and inspiration. We nurture our authors so that their stories can unfurl on the page, helping them to share their uplifting and moving stories.

Cherish Editions is unique in that a percentage of the profits from the sale of our books goes directly to leading mental health charity Shawmind, to deliver its vision to provide support for those experiencing mental ill health.

Find out more about Cherish Editions by visiting cherisheditions.com or joining us on:

Twitter @cherisheditions
Facebook @cherisheditions
Instagram @cherisheditions

Cherish
EDITIONS

ABOUT SHAWMIND

A proportion of profits from the sale of all Trigger books go to their sister charity, Shawmind, also founded by Adam Shaw and Lauren Callaghan. The charity aims to ensure that everyone has access to mental health resources whenever they need them.

Find out more about the work Shawmind do by visiting shawmind.org or joining them on:

Twitter @Shawmind_
Facebook @ShawmindUK
Instagram @Shawmind_

Your Local Mental Health & Wellbeing Charity

Printed in the USA
CPSIA information can be obtained
at www.ICGtesting.com
LVHW03081803102 3
759781LV00099B/3265

9 781915 680617